WHILE YOU WERE SLEEPING

FUN FACTS THAT HAPPEN EVERY NIGHT

Steve Murrie & Matthew Murrie
Illustrated by **Tom Bloom**

SCHOLASTIC

Z Z Z Z Z Acknowledgments

I'd like to thank my wife, Seung Ah Lee, and my wonderful family for all of their support. A huge thank you to Jessica Regel, our agent, who never stops looking for new opportunities to help us put our ideas onto paper. Thank you to Brenda Murray, our longtime editor at Scholastic, who gave us our first shot and hasn't given up on us yet. A special thanks to Christopher Hernandez, who showed an inordinate amount of patience as he edited this work and made sure that we got it all right. I'd also like to thank all of the people at Westminster College who have provided me with an ideal environment to complete a book like this, especially my students who had to deal with the ups and downs of a professor writing a book. Thank you to my emergency mathematician, Hashish Hoassam. And thank you to all the people from all over the world who have opened my eyes to the immense totality of this planet and have placed me in constant amazement of its awesomeness.

—Matthew Murrie

A special thanks to the following, without whom this book (along with the rest of our books) would not have been possible: God's grace; Nancy for the title, proofreading, suggestions, and support; Dan, Holli, Libby, and Andrew for their support; Jack, Will, Caroline, and Grant for the joy they bring; our editors, Brenda Murray and Chris Hernandez, for their guidance; and our agent, Jessica Regel, for her hard work and dedication.

—Steve Murrie

Contents

ZZZZz # Introduction

What if you never slept? WHAT IF YOU STAYED AWAKE ALL DAY AND NIGHT? Would you get too tired to enjoy your life?

Even though you're not awake for it, sleep is one of the most important things you'll do in life. If you get the recommended seven to eight hours of sleep every night, you'll wind up sleeping about one third of your life. Even though your eyes are closed and your mind drifts off to dreamland, your body is still busy doing work to make sure you can function to your fullest while you're awake. In order to keep your body feeling fine, don't forget your bedtime.

But your body isn't the only thing with stuff to do while you're asleep at night. There's an entire universe of activity going on. For people stuck on Earth, most of what's in space can only be seen at night. And those space objects are growing, collapsing, observing, and doing things we're not even sure about. Back on Earth, some people are just beginning their workday at night, activities necessary to keep the world functioning are occurring, and don't forget, our Sun can't shine on us all at the same time; when one side of the globe is going to sleep, the other side is just waking up. And for many living creatures with which we share the planet, the nighttime is their time. Whether it's because it's too dangerous to be seen in the daytime for fear of being eaten, or because the tastiest treats only come out at night, many animals choose to sleep in all day and go out all night. Several plants (like the moonflower) and natural occurrences also wait until night to display their splendor.

It is our hope that this book will turn your world on its head before you go to bed. By reading it, we hope you can no longer look at your bedtime as a march toward the end of the day, but rather just the beginning to the many wonderful things about to start the moment your head hits your pillow.

May all of your dreams be filled with wonder so your days are never dull.

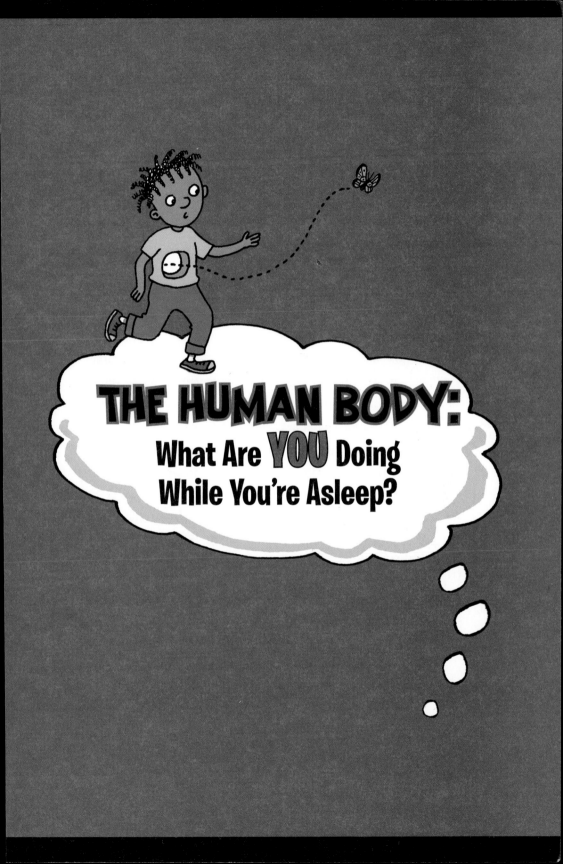

THE HUMAN BODY:
What Are YOU Doing While You're Asleep?

ZzZzz The Brain

News flash! The human brain does NOT turn off when we go to bed at night. There is evidence that suggests it may be nearly as active at night while we're sleeping as when we're awake during the day. Humans have four well-known kinds of brain waves, each representing a different speed of electrical activity in the brain. Delta waves are the slowest, then theta waves; alpha waves are faster, and beta waves are the fastest of the bunch. Typically, only beta and alpha waves are active when we're awake. When we go to bed, our brains shift from beta waves to alpha waves as we begin to relax, slowing down to delta once we've zonked out. But our brains don't stay relaxed for the entire night. Every 90 minutes or so of sleep, our brains have a spike of activity during the process of rapid eye movement (REM), in which our eyes dart around and we have dreams . . . or nightmares!

Everybody Dreams

But do BLIND PEOPLE dream?
Of course! Dreams are such a powerful and important
part of our lives that even the lack of sight can't stop one's
dreams. What kind of dreams does someone who can't see
have? Blind sleepers have reported that they can see as much
and as well in their dreams as they could before they lost their
sight. In their dreams, friends and family appear the same as they
last saw them, without aging. In cases in which the dreamers
were born blind, they have what's called an auditory dream: a
dream without images, but full of sounds.

Zzzzz Brain Napping

Don't you wish your parents would let you STAY UP ALL NIGHT playing video games and watching television? Bet you think you would hit that new high score if you could just play a few more hours a day. But, believe it or not, having a bedtime is actually much more helpful. Scientists have observed that in brains that haven't had enough sleep, nerves can temporarily go off-line. Even more strangely, this will happen while the rest of the brain remains awake. The result of these brain naps? Forgetfulness, putting things in the wrong place, and mislaunched Angry Birds. A full night's sleep means a full day's play.

Body Temperature

SLEEPING IS COOL. No, really. When you sleep, your body temperature actually drops nearly 2°F (1°C) to help you fall into a deeper sleep. The deeper you sleep, the more work your body can do to maintain a healthy you, such as recharging your brain, building muscles, and regulating your chemicals. The connection between your dropping body temperature and sleep is so strong, some doctors recommend taking a hot bath an hour and a half before bedtime for people who have difficulty sleeping. The sudden drop in temperature from getting out of the bath could be enough to trigger the body into believing it's bedtime.

Zzzzz Skin

We don't mean to give you nightmares, but you should know **YOUR SKIN IS DEAD.** At least, the top layer is, anyway. This layer of skin is really just a bunch of dead cells. Gross, right? Your body spends most of the day shedding these cells by the thousands. How are your living skin cells replaced? Through your beauty sleep, of course! One of the many jobs your body gets to work on during the night is the repairing of tissue damage done to your skin as a result of its daylong exposure to the sun and pollution in the air.

Heart

Even though exciting dreams—
or nightmares—might make you
think your heart is racing, your
HEART SLOWS DOWN
while you are sleeping. On average,
a person's heart slows down by 12 beats per minute.
That may not sound like much, but doing so significantly
lowers your blood pressure, which, in turn, decreases
the opportunity for calcium to build up in your arteries.
Isn't calcium good for you? It's great for bones, but too
much in your blood vessels can lead to heart attacks.
This effect doesn't happen overnight, which is why
getting plenty of sleep when you're young is helpful for
having a healthy heart when you're older.

Muscles

Can sleeping make you stronger? Believe it or not, a good night's sleep could be the **BEST (AND EASIEST) WORKOUT** you'll ever have.

Sleep is an important part of every exercise regime, but not because of the workout you receive from all that tossing and turning, which is an average of 35 times a night. It's what your muscles are allowed to do only when you're not moving that counts. While you are sleeping, your body can repair the muscle tissue that's torn from exercising. Without these necessary repairs, it would be difficult for the muscles to grow. When you're awake, well-rested muscles are also able to work out more.

Breathing

Of course **YOU** don't snore, nobody thinks **THEY** snore. But why do other people snore? Because their muscles are resting. More specifically, the muscles in their throats are relaxing while the snorers are sleeping. How can taking it easy be so noisy? When the snorer's throat muscles relax, the airways in their throat become narrower. As a result, the air that passes through when they breathe causes their uvula (the finger-looking thing dangling down from the back of their mouth) and soft palate (the back of the roof of their mouth) to vibrate. Those vibrations are usually the snores you hear.

Z Z Z Z Z Mouth (Saliva)

Ever wake up with a dry mouth? No, it's not caused by DREAMING ABOUT THE DESERT. It's because your mouth slows down its production of saliva when you're asleep. Saliva is extremely important for the digestion of food, but not that necessary while you're sleeping. Therefore, in order to make sure your saliva glands are well rested and ready to flow when you're awake, your body makes less saliva while you're sleeping. Sleeping with your mouth open can make things even drier, so if you wake up feeling like you were chewing on chalk all night, try sleeping with your mouth closed, or keep a glass of water next to your bed.

Digestive System

While you are sleeping, one of the biggest, most energy-consuming systems in your body also gets to TAKE IT EASY —your digestive system.

It takes much more than just your stomach to break down all of the food you eat. There are several organs that work to break down food into energy your body can use. Keeping all of the involved organs working properly takes up oodles of your body's energy. Although your digestive system never completely shuts off, sleeping gives it the opportunity to slow down so it can be well rested in time for breakfast.

Zzzzz Bacteria Breath

While eating a garlic and anchovy pizza would certainly give you BREATH BAD ENOUGH TO KEEP VAMPIRES AWAY, did you know sleep also affects your breath? Bad breath comes from microscopic bacteria living in our mouths. The gas these uninvited guests give off causes that stinky smell. *Gross!* Every mouth is home to roughly 100 types of bacteria, and they love our mouths while we're sleeping because it is when our mouths are the driest. What can help? Sleep with your mouth closed to keep it from getting too dry and to keep from breathing in more bacteria from the air. Flossing and brushing your teeth before going to bed are other ways to make sure your bacteria behave.

Immune System

A full night's sleep is even **BETTER THAN AN APPLE** at keeping the doctor away. Studies show that missing just a few hours of sleep can cause your immune system to *cause* illness. Not sleeping enough can trigger inflammation that damages healthy tissue, thus causing this system that is meant to protect you from sickness to harm your healthy organs and tissue. One long-term result is an increased risk of catching colds or flus. An even longer-term consequence of not sleeping enough is an increased risk of heart disease. And if you do get sick, your sleep becomes even more important, as proper sleep allows your body to fight off colds and infections.

Z Z Z Z Z

Bile Produced

Your gallbladder plays an important part in a healthy digestive system, but it's got to wait for you to stop eating to STORE UP ITS SPECIAL SAUCE, better known as bile. While you're sleeping, your gallbladder is busy storing bile for later. Bile is a concoction of salts, acids, and other molecules that help your body digest the fat you eat. Fat is like oil; your body is about 60 percent water. Ever try to mix oil and water? It doesn't work. Without bile, your body wouldn't be able to transport fat out of your body; it would just stay where it is. Bile transforms all that fat floating around into fatty acids. Unlike pure fat, fatty acids are something your body can get rid of, and after your body gets rid of them, you get rid of them when you flush the toilet.

Nighttime Nails

HATE CUTTING YOUR NAILS? Get more sleep. Even

though your finger and toenails are constantly growing—
about 0.004 inches (0.1 millimeters) every day—they
slow down when you're sleeping. The nails on your
dominant hand also grow faster than on your other hand.
Increased blood circulation while you're awake helps
contribute to nail growth, but so does being more active.
Trauma, or damage, to your fingertips and nails signals
your body to accelerate growth. Since nails are for
protection, trauma tricks your body into thinking your
nails need to be replaced. While sleeping, your nails
experience very little trauma, so your body believes they
are safe.

Zzzz To Sleep or Not to Sleep?

You don't just have to fight with your parents to stay awake at night—you also have to **FIGHT WITH YOURSELF!** Inside of your brain, there is a never-ending battle waged over whether you stay awake or go to sleep. Parts of your brain stem and hypothalamus (a region of your brain) deliver signals to your body telling you to stay awake, while another part of your hypothalamus sends out different signals prompting your body to shut down and go to sleep. These changes in signals can happen so quickly that when you go to sleep, you do so in mere seconds.

White Blood Cells Produced

If getting sick were against the law, your white blood cells would be **YOUR BODY'S ELITE CRIME-FIGHTING TEAM.** There are actually three types of white blood cells: granulocytes, monocytes, and lymphocytes—but as a group, they are known as leukocytes. These microscopic cells pack quite a punch against infections, but their strength is in their numbers. Your body produces around 120,000 white blood cells every second! Current studies are indicating that our sleep greatly affects our production of white blood cells. Not sleeping enough when you're healthy can end up making you sick, and getting a full night's sleep when you are sick is like calling for backup when you have a bunch of tiny bad guys trying to keep you that way.

Blood Pumped

Fortunately for you, YOUR HEART NEVER RESTS. That means, even when you get tired and shut your eyes at night, it keeps pumping and pumping. Your heart gets to slow down while you're sleeping, because it's easier to send blood to your entire body when you're flat as a board. On average, a grown person pumps around 2,000 gallons (7,570 liters) of blood around his or her body in a day. That means your heart is pumping blood at a rate of roughly 83 gallons (314 liters) per hour down your internal interstate blood-way! But that's during the day. Once you go to sleep, your heart rate slows down by about 8 percent.

Internal Clock

TICKTOCK, TICKTOCK . . .

that's not your alarm clock, it's your internal clock. You may want to stay awake or go to sleep, but it's not up to *you*. Actually, it's up to some very small parts of you: About 50,000 cells located in your brain's suprachiasmatic nucleus (SCN) help determine whether you go to sleep or stay awake. When your eyes are exposed to light—even if they're closed—they send signals to your SCN to reset your "sleep clock" to **AWAKE**. Throughout the day, your SCN produces an alerting signal to the rest of your brain to keep you from going to sleep. Your SCN then begins a new countdown timer that will later shut off that alerting signal, allowing you to fall back asleep.

Z Z Z Z Human Growth Hormone Produced

BIGGER, FASTER, SLEEPIER?

Athletes are known to do anything they can to get a competitive edge. But you don't have to cheat to improve your performance; you just have to get enough sleep. Even though injecting yourself with human growth hormone (HGH) is now banned in most professional sports, your body still produces it naturally. The pituitary gland, where HGH is made, waits until you are in your deepest stage of sleep to release HGH throughout your body. No wonder athletes try to increase their levels of HGH, since it is responsible for growing and maintaining muscles, strengthening bones, decreasing body fat, and helping the heart. But too much can be dangerous—remember, your body knows best.

Can You Smell and Sleep at the Same Time?

z z z z

SMOKE ALARMS CAN BE LIFESAVERS when a fire occurs in the middle of the night. Not because you are too sleepy to wake up during a fire, but because you can't smell the toxic fumes in the smoke. Many believe people can't smell in their sleep, but this is a myth. You *can* smell in your sleep, but people have a hard time waking up from the smell of fire because smoke from a fire gives off an odorless, poisonous gas that can get to you before the smell of smoke—or the heat of fire—reaches you. Once this gas gets to you, it's strong enough to keep you asleep.

Your Nightly Nervous System

There are so many functions needed to keep you alive that your body NEVER FULLY GOES TO SLEEP. Since it would be impossible for you to constantly remember to tell your heart to pump, your lungs to breathe, and your stomach to digest your lunch, your body takes care of these functions all by itself. This autopilot is your nervous system. Your nervous system can be divided up into two main parts: sympathetic and parasympathetic systems. The biggest difference between the two is when they take over. When you're active, the sympathetic system rules your nerves, slowing down your digestion and increasing your heartbeats so you can stay alert and busy. Your parasympathetic system does just the opposite, helping your body conserve energy so it can digest your food. Maybe that's why a nap sounds so good right after eating a big meal.

You're Getting Sleepy . . . Very Sleepy

You might think that SLEEP IS SLEEP, but that's not true. In fact, there are five distinct stages your brain goes through during sleep. The deeper your sleep, the more your muscle movement slows and eventually, the more active your brain becomes. The first stage of sleep is one of extremely light sleep, then you gradually go into deeper and deeper sleep. Sleep during the first stage is so light that you might not even realize you are sleeping. By the time you reach the fifth stage of sleep, your brain has become very active and your voluntary muscles have become paralyzed. It is during this final stage of sleep, known as rapid eye movement (REM), that most of your dreams take place. That's why your muscles have to shut down—so you can't act out your dreams.

Zzzzz Dreaming Your Life Away

Has anyone ever called you a dreamer? Don't worry; **YOU'RE NOT THE ONLY ONE.** We all dream.

In fact, during a typical 8-hour sleep, the average person will drift off into **REM** sleep (the stage of sleep in which dreams take place) five times. So, in one year, you're likely to have around 1,825 dreams! By the time you reach 75, you'll have over 136,875 dreams. No wonder we have such a hard time remembering every dream we have.

A Brain Trilogy

When you're asleep, three parts of the brain WORK ALL NIGHT to affect how you dream. Starting in the lower section of the brain, your brain stem pauses all of your muscle movements, except for the muscles of your eyes. In doing so, you fall into rapid eye movement (REM) sleep. REM sleep is when most dreams happen. Once you start dreaming, your middle brain gets active. This section of the brain is responsible for emotions, which explains how dreams can be so pleasurable or so haunting. The last part of your brain, your higher brain, while not shut off completely, is more or less taking a nap through most of your dreams. This part of your brain is where your critical thinking and reasoning come from. Its inactivity explains how you are able to believe that the monsters in your dreams are real.

Red Blood Cell Production

BLOOD: IT'S NOT JUST FOR VAMPIRES.

Your body needs it, too. More specifically, it's what's in the blood that you need. One of the most important things in your blood are red blood cells. If blood vessels are like streets in your body, then red blood cells would be buses giving rides, carrying passengers of oxygen and carbon dioxide. As red blood cells pass through your lungs, they pick up oxygen and transport it to tissue all over your body. After dropping off oxygen, the cells pick up carbon dioxide and other waste, and transport them away from your healthy tissue. Your body is constantly producing new red blood cells. In fact, it's producing 2 million new red blood cells every second. That's just under 58 *billion* produced during a good night's sleep!

Sleep Peeing

How often do you go 8 hours or more during the day without making A TRIP TO THE BATHROOM? Probably not too often. So how are you able to sleep 8 or more hours at night without leaving your bedroom for your bathroom? Fortunately for you, your body understands how important uninterrupted sleep is for your health and happiness. While your body releases a special hormone called vasopressin throughout the day, it releases more of it at night. While you are sleeping, this hormone helps reduce your body's production of urine to less than what it produces during the day. That way, your bladder doesn't fill up as fast, so your sleep can last.

ZzZzz From Sleep to Sleep

Can getting some sleep help you get some sleep? Sounds strange, BUT IT'S TRUE.

One of the ways your body regulates its sleep patterns is by producing the sleeping-inducing hormone melatonin. Not only is melatonin released during the evening and into the night, but your body also *waits* to produce it until after the sun goes down. This is why melatonin is nicknamed the "Dracula of hormones"—it only comes out at night. Your body doesn't store melatonin, so it must make more every evening. If you don't get enough sleep at night, your body might not create enough melatonin for you to get a restful sleep. So, be sure to go to sleep at night . . . so you can sleep at night. Sounds simple, huh?

Turn It Off to Turn Sleep On

Wouldn't it be great if you could STAY UP ALL NIGHT and not have to sleep?

Think how much work you'd get done . . . or how much television you could watch. Whether you like it or not, your body has a built-in system to make sure you get your sleep. A small gland in your brain, called the pineal gland, secretes a chemical called melatonin that makes you sleepy. The amount of melatonin in your body starts to increase late in the evening, and then maxes out during the night to keep you dozed off; it lets up again in the morning. If you're having trouble falling asleep, experts suggest turning off the television or computer at least an hour before bedtime, because the glow from electronic devices can disrupt your melatonin production.

No Crying in Your Sleep

You may have cried yourself to sleep before, but you didn't do any crying AFTER YOU WERE ASLEEP—it's far more difficult. As a part of your body's nightly transfer of energy from daytime functions to nighttime repairs, your production of tears stops almost entirely. How do your eyeballs keep from turning into a couple of raisins by the time you wake up? Another function of falling asleep is for your eyelids to form a watertight seal over your eyes. That way, all of the moisture on your eyes before you go to sleep will remain there until you wake up, keeping your eyes from drying out overnight.

Go to Bed Already!

Have you ever stayed up all night without going to sleep? How about **TWO NIGHTS IN A ROW?**

Three nights? It's doubtful you could stay awake for more than a single night because your body wants sleep, and it's willing to fight you for it. If you try to stop your body from sleeping, it has some pretty strange ways to let you know it's tired. While a history of sleepless nights can seriously damage your long-term health, not sleeping tonight could make you forget things, or even see things, tomorrow. Two of the most common side effects of short-term sleep deprivation are forgetfulness and hallucinations. What's the longest someone ever went without sleep? In 1965, Randy Gardner stayed awake for 11 days as a part of his high school science fair.

A Stomach Full of Acid

While acid can turn regular people into NIGHTMARISH VILLAINS in comic books, we're all carrying around a whole stomach full of the stuff. While you're fast asleep, your stomach is dissolving whatever you ate during the day. In order to do so, it relies on the acid to break the food down from solid chunks to something your body can digest and turn into energy. To be clear, this acid is really powerful—not only does it dissolve food, it also dissolves the lining of your stomach. So your body uses its superpowers to regenerate a new stomach lining every 3 to 4 days.

The Smells Dreams Are Made Of

z z z Z Z

Could your NOSE be a pathway into your dreams? New studies on sleep, smell, and dreams suggest that what you smell while you're asleep might also affect what sort of dreams you have. As strange as it sounds, bad smells may lead to bad dreams. In one study, sleepers were given smells of rotten eggs or fresh-cut roses. Guess which ones had more pleasant dreams? Even though the sleepers didn't report any particular smells in their dreams, nice smells created nice dreams and rotten eggs caused rotten dreams.

Sleep: It Does Your Brain Good

GO TO SLEEP TONIGHT

to help your body—and brain—tomorrow. Not only does sleep help your body rebuild muscles and tissues, it also helps your brain form. When you're young, your body isn't the sole thing growing and changing, so is your brain. Scientists now believe that while you're sleeping, the frontal lobe develops connections to the rest of your brain. A fully developed frontal lobe is important, because it's the part of the brain that helps us make better long-term decisions and control our impulses later on in life. *The first impulse to control now in order to make sure your brain is fully functional later?* Shutting off your phone or computer before bedtime and getting 8-10 hours of sleep . . . *every* night.

Don't Live Your Dreams

The best thing about dreams is that you can go just about anywhere and do just about anything WITHOUT EVER LEAVING YOUR BED.

But have you ever wondered how you're able to think and feel as if you're moving around without actually doing it? The secret comes from a portion of your brain called the pons. Before your dreams begin, the pons sends signals to shut off neurons in your spinal cord. Doing so temporarily paralyzes your muscles. That way, you don't have to get out of bed to fly through the clouds in your dream. However, there are people who suffer from REM sleep behavior disorder (RBD). It can be very dangerous to fall asleep next to someone with RBD, since he or she may spend many nights punching, kicking, yelling, and jumping out of bed.

Your Brain, Your Blood, Your Sleep

Your brain is ONE GREEDY ORGAN. Even though it makes up only 2 percent of your body, it requires up to 25 percent of your blood—while you're awake. Once you go to sleep, it takes a blood break. While you're sleeping, your brain merely gets about 60 percent of the blood it gets while you're awake. Where does that blood go, if not to your brain? It goes to the rest of your body, mainly your muscles, for repairs and to restore energy. However, if you get fewer hours of sleep than you need, your muscles cannot be fully repaired, since your body doesn't have as much time to produce the necessary human growth hormone to build back your muscles.

Sleep for Strength

Testosterone is a steroid hormone that helps **BUILD MUSCLES,** increase bone mass, and grow **BODY HAIR.** While both males and females produce testosterone, males produce about 10 to 20 times more than females do. However, the testosterone of *both* males and females is greatly affected by sleep. A person's testosterone level naturally rises when asleep and lowers when awake. Doctors have recently discovered that people who don't get enough sleep also experience lower levels of testosterone. Getting a good night's sleep might just be the easiest way to get stronger—and hairier!

zzzzzSleepwalking

Have you ever gone to bed only to get back OUT OF BED . . . without even knowing it? Even if you can't remember doing it, there's a good chance you've been sleepwalking before—or have laughed at or been startled by someone else who was. The scientific name for sleepwalking is *somnambulism,* and it's actually quite common in children. Sleepwalking typically occurs within the first hour or two of falling asleep and can last anywhere from a few seconds to half an hour. Luckily, most kids tend to grow out of it by the time they reach their teens. Good thing, too—we wouldn't want anyone sleep driving!

Are You SAD?

Sure, most people probably prefer the **SUNSHINE OF SUMMER** to the cold and **DARKNESS OF WINTER,** but some people actually suffer from a lack of sunshine. Calling it Seasonal Affective Disorder (SAD), doctors now have a name for the depression many people feel only during certain times of the year. A lack of sunlight has been shown to affect people's sleep-wake cycle and might also affect how the brain releases certain mood-changing chemicals, like serotonin. Your body relies on sunlight to let it know when and how long to stay asleep. The long, dark days of winter can keep your body from knowing when to sleep and when to stay awake. This lack of sunlight can cause people to want to sleep more than they normally would and to feel down when they're awake.

ZzZzZz Bristlemouth Fish

Would you believe that one of the world's BIGGEST MIGRATIONS occurs every single night? These millions and millions of migrating animals are deep-sea fish, including jellyfish, lantern fish, and giant squid, which rise from the depths of the world's oceans, known as the twilight zone. Some members of this group travel up to 3,280 feet (1,000 meters) from their deep daytime hangouts in the ocean depths to feed on the many smaller fish that live closer to the surface. The bristlemouth fish are the most numerous among this massive migrating group. The bristlemouth gets its name from the sharp, brushlike teeth that stick out from its mouth.

(In)Active Armadillos

Experts recommend 8 hours of sleep every night, which would make the armadillo an **OVERACHIEVER**—it gets 16 hours of sleep! But not at night—instead, it's awake during those 8 hours you're asleep. How does it spend its evenings? Eating and avoiding cars. Armadillos use their supersticky tongues to eat up to 40,000 ants in a single meal. Since they sleep during the day, most armadillos you see will be ones taking permanent naps on the sides of roads. While they have noses strong enough to smell ants, their eyesight is awful . . . and it's hard to smell a car coming.

Zzzz Tasmanian Devil

"SHHH! I'M TRYING TO SLEEP." **Try telling that to a Tasmanian devil.** These little devils' voices are so bloodcurdlingly frightening, they're responsible for the negative name. It was given to them by European settlers in Tasmania, Australia, who were often woken up at night to the devilish screams and screeches the feisty demons make when tearing into their late-night meals. There's little doubt they can be mean, though: They have the third-most-powerful bite of all animals, and their ears turn a bright red when they get excited. They even have to live alone, because they can't get along with other devils.

Honey Badger

Not sure you want to go to sleep at night? **YOU'RE NOT ALONE.** The honey badger spends its summers sleeping during the day and its winters sleeping at night. It might have a sweet-smelling name, but this badger really stinks. Good luck staying asleep if one of these decides to drop a liquid stink bomb next to you. And if its smell isn't enough to scare you away, its appetite should. These guys will eat almost anything, from tiny insects to smaller crocodiles and, of course, honey. But it's not the honey they're after; it's the juicy bee larvae inside the hive. What about all of those bees? The honey badger doesn't care. Its skin is so thick, it is protected from bee stings.

Z Z Z z z **Wombat**

Ever been told you're as "WISE AS A WOMBAT"? Probably not, but a group of wombats is referred to as a wisdom. Actually, wombats aren't known for being wise; they're known for their digging. Able to move 3 feet (1 meter) of dirt in a single night as they dig tunnels underground, wombats are the largest burrowing mammals on the planet. When they're not digging, they're grazing 3-8 hours a night. Not because they love staying awake all night, but because it's cool. Since wombats prefer cool temperatures, they wisely wait to sleep when it's hot. When temperatures drop, don't be surprised to see a wombat during the day, doing—what else? Digging.

Wolverine

EVEN WILD ANIMALS HAVE NIGHTMARES about wolverines. Ferocious as they are fearless, these unfriendly predators have been known to break into burrows uninvited to feast on much larger mammals while they hibernate. Even though wolverines hunt mostly at night, few things—much less daylight—will keep them from enjoying a meaty meal. They've even been known to wander as far as 30 miles (48 kilometers) in a single day just for a snack. Until they grow mean enough to scare off a bear, baby wolverines (called kits) are white to blend in with the snow of their surroundings.

Z Z Z Z Z Red Panda

Do you have a FAVORITE BLANKET you can't sleep without?

If so, you're not alone. The red panda carries its "blanky" with it everywhere it goes, too. But it has to; its favorite blanket is also its tail. Like most animals with tails, the red panda uses its long tail for balance while running or resting across treetops. When daylight comes and it's time to go to sleep, it curls its extra-bushy tail around and snuggles its face in it to keep itself warm from the cool mountain air of its environment.

Hedgehog

Ever wake up after a night of **TOSSING AND TURNING** **with your hair all messy?** No amount of showering can tame a hedgehog's "bed head." But its bad hair is also its best defense. Hedgehogs use their quills, which are made of keratin (the same material as your hair and fingernails) to protect themselves from predators by curling into a spike-covered ball whenever they are threatened. They also do this when they fall asleep. And if being pointy weren't enough, hedgehogs make their quills poisonous by eating toxic plants and then licking the quills: an ideal defense for animals with poor eyesight that roam around at night.

ANIMALS

Z Z Z Z Z Fennec Fox

Weighing just 2.2 pounds (1 kilogram), the fennec fox might be the TINIEST FOX IN THE WORLD, but it isn't "crazy like a fox." Living in a desert environment, it does its best to avoid the heat by sleeping all day underground. Then, when the desert sun goes down, the fox comes out to hunt. Wouldn't AC be easier? Who needs air-conditioning when you've got ears nearly a quarter of the size of your whole body? Huh? Not only do the fennec fox's large, powerful ears allow it to hear critters crawling underground, they also help the fox by radiating heat away from its body. These large ears spread out, providing extra space for heat to go—far away from the rest of the fox's body.

ZzZZZ

Tokay Gecko

Believe it or not, some geckos really do work for humans. But they don't **WAKE UP EVERY MORNING TO GO TO AN OFFICE** as you may have seen on TV. Instead, the tokay gecko wakes up every *night* to go to "work" when most people are going to bed. Pest control is this lizard's line of work. They're so famous for getting rid of cockroaches and other pests, people consider them to be good luck. And if it runs into any bad luck of its own, it will detach its own tail! But that's not all: The tail twists and turns as if it's alive, fooling any predator in pursuit, while the gecko makes a quick getaway.

ZZZZZ Earthworm

Do you know what GROSS CREATURES come out at night to feed and are commonly referred to as night crawlers? No, they're not zombies or vampires—although too much sunlight *is* deadly for them. These slimy slitherers are earthworms, and they do what they can to avoid the sun, from burrowing deep underground to coming out only at night. Just an hour in the sun is enough to paralyze a worm, causing it to get stuck in place to roast or become bird food. Why would they ever come out to see the light of day? Because when it rains, the ground can get so full of water that they'd drown if they stayed beneath the surface.

Duck-Billed Platypus

How long would you sleep if you could close your eyes AND your ears? The duck-billed platypus can do just that, but it doesn't close them to sleep; it closes its eyes and ears when swimming to keep the water out. These crepuscular, or twilight-dwelling, swimmers are most often seen very early in the morning or very late at night, and they don't swim for fun: They swim for food. How does one find its lunch with its eyes and ears closed? The ducklike bill on the front of their face is sensitive to electrical signals in the bodies of other swimmers. Swimming around with its eyes and ears closed must be tiring because the platypus spends up to 14 hours a day sleeping.

Z Z Z Z Z Red-Eyed Tree Frog

The red-eyed tree frog can rest easily during the day because its BRIGHT GREEN COLOR MAKES IT NEARLY INVISIBLE when getting lazy on a leaf. Sleeping all day means this frog is highly active at night. Whenever it's in danger, it knows how to spook its enemies. Opening its bright red eyes can be enough to scare away a striking predator. Or it can just jump. Jumping exposes the frog's bright blue legs. This quick flash of color can create a blur like a ghost. So, even if the "ghost" doesn't scare the predator away, the predator will bite into nothing but air.

Snowy Owl

It's unfortunate **OWLS DON'T DELIVER THE MAIL** because the snowy owl would be the perfect animal to do so: No amount of bad weather seems to deter it. It survives in one of the harshest environments on Earth: the Arctic. Unlike other owls, the snowy owl doesn't come out at night to hunt. Since the Arctic experiences 24 hours of daylight during summer months, it can't avoid the light. And it doesn't need magic to keep warm during the winter, when there's 24 hours of darkness; it uses its abundance of feathers—even on its bill and toes—to keep warm.

Z z z z z Bush Baby

All babies are AFRAID OF THE DARK, right? Not bush babies.

They come out at night because they have good reason to be afraid of the light. They're so tiny—and tasty—they need to hide during the *day* to keep from being eaten by eagles, snakes, or even chimpanzees. They spend the daytime sleeping inside tree hollows and use the night's darkness as protection when they come out to eat. Luckily for bush babies, they have extra-large eyes that help them see in the dark. How do these "babies" get their name if they aren't afraid of the dark? Their cries sound a lot like a human baby's.

Vampire Bat

Z Z Z Z Z

All vampires might prefer the nighttime to daytime, but NOT ALL VAMPIRES SUCK. True to its name, the vampire bat comes out only at night. And it does live completely off the blood of others. Weighing between 0.5 and 1.7 ounces (15 and 50 grams), it drinks about half of its weight in blood every night. But these furry vampires never suck blood. Instead, they cut their prey with their teeth, and carefully lick the blood up with their tiny tongues. In keeping with vampires' impeccable grooming habits, these bats regularly groom themselves and have been known to give regurgitated blood to other bats in exchange for their grooming services.

ZZzzz Coyote

Could you switch from sleeping at NIGHT to sleeping all DAY?

Many coyotes had to find out if they could, in order to survive. Luckily for the coyotes, they're survivor specialists. Coyotes can be found all over North America: in mountains, deserts, forests, prairies, even in suburbs and cities. Most coyotes in the wild sleep at night and hunt during the day, but scientists have learned that the closer coyotes live to humans, the longer they stay up at night and the more they snooze during the day. They do this in order to coexist with larger human populations—what would you do if you saw a pack of coyotes wandering around on your way to school? Staying out of the sight of humans helps them stay alive. What other survival technique do coyotes use to live in cities? They've developed a taste for garbage.

Scorpion

Ever been **TOO COLD TO FALL ASLEEP?** Even though they live primarily in warm climates, scorpions aren't too picky about the temperature when it comes to sleeping. Some have been frozen overnight and lived to walk away the next day. Of course, no scorpion would choose to spend the *night* in a freezer—they prefer staying awake all night. Even though they sleep during the day and aren't choosy about the temperature, they've made it known their preference is to be awake in the dark. Where scorpions are plentiful, it's not uncommon to wake up finding one sleeping in one's shoe or pant leg.

ANIMALS

Aye-Aye

If you looked like a **MASH-UP OF A LEMUR AND AN ELECTROCUTED KOALA,** you'd probably come out only at night, too. Fortunately for an aye-aye in Madagascar, it can survive just fine in the dark. Rather than using its big bug eyes to find food, it taps on trees and uses its batlike ears to listen for insects inside. Once it locates their movements, it sticks one of its long, skinny fingers in to dig out its late-night lunch. It's lucky that the aye-ayes come out only at night; many people of Madagascar consider them to be bad luck.

Clouded Leopard

Called a mint leopard in China, tree tiger in Malaysia, and clouded leopard by English speakers, this cat's name **ISN'T THE ONLY THING** that's clouded about it. It can't even decide when to sleep. Where there are no other large cats around, it sleeps mostly at night and hunts during the day. However, when there are larger leopards around, it spends its days sleeping up high in the branches of trees. Unlike other jungle cats, the clouded leopard can hang upside down from branches by its hind legs, as a monkey does. And when it does come down at night to hunt, it climbs down headfirst, more like a squirrel than a cat.

Spring Peeper

Ever **FEEL LIKE SINGING** once winter is finally over? Spring peeper frogs get their name from all the singing they do at the beginning of spring. Yet as easy as they are to hear, they're tough to see. When you're about 1 inch (2.5 centimeters) long fully grown, and you can't help bursting out in song, it's important to take every precaution to keep from getting gobbled up by predators. That's why they come out only at night, to feast on spiders and insects. The skin of the spring peepers also changes color to match their surroundings: lightening as the sun goes down and brightening back up when the sun returns.

Dark Fishing Spider

The dark fishing spider's **NAME SAYS IT ALL.** Spending all day resting in dark places, it waits until night to come out. Rather than spinning a web and waiting for insects to fly in and get stuck, it likes to go on the hunt . . . er . . . go fishing. It can, literally, walk on water. And it uses this special ability to find its prey. While insects living near water are its most common meal, it has been known to catch small fish as well. If it gets scared while fishing, it can even dive below the surface of the water to hide.

Zzzzz Flying Squirrel

IT'S A BIRD . . . IT'S A PLANE . . . IT'S A SQUIRREL?

Rather than scurrying around the ground like other squirrels, the flying squirrel looks down on its furry cousins as it sails through the sky, at distances of over 150 feet (46 meters). The flying squirrel doesn't really fly, though. Instead, it spreads out the large folds of skin connected between its legs to keep it afloat in the air, after jumping from high up. Good luck spotting one in flight; flying squirrels could probably add the word *stealth* to their name since they take to the skies only at night.

Kangaroo Rat

Z Z Z Z Z

Deserts can be **TOUGH PLACES** to survive. The lack of water and extreme heat are the biggest challenges. But they can't keep the kangaroo rat from surviving. It's tough to live in a place with as little water as a desert, but luckily, the kangaroo rat gets enough moisture from the seeds it eats. Since it consumes so little water, it can't even sweat. It solves this problem by sleeping the hot desert days away in underground burrows, coming out only at night when it's cool. How does it get the *kangaroo* in its name? It's an excellent jumper—it can leap 9 feet (2.8 meters)—and it has a pair of pouches on the outsides of its cheeks to hold extra food.

ZZZZZ Luna Moth

There's no **MIDNIGHT SNACK** for the luna moth—it doesn't even have a mouth! This nighttime flier doesn't really need to eat since it lives only for about a week. Before it's a moth, it crawls on trees as a plump, green caterpillar. To transform into a moth, the caterpillar spins a cocoon and takes a 2-3-week nap inside; if it makes its cocoon close to winter, it will stay inside until early spring. When it crawls out, it must hang its wings down to fill them up with blood before it can fly. Once they're filled, it waits until nightfall to take flight.

Lion

Lions neither live **IN THE JUNGLE** nor do they always **SLEEP AT NIGHT.** But they are mighty, especially the lionesses, or female lions. Male lions might have better hairdos but, compared to lionesses, they're pretty lazy. In a pride of lions, it's the lionesses that come out to do most of the hunting. The lionesses use stealth, speed, strength, and teamwork to take down animals as large as an elephant. But when they bring home the "hippo bacon," it's the males that get to eat first, since they're bigger. One lion can eat up to 60 pounds (27 kilograms) in a single meal!

Zzzz Koala

Ever get tired of eating THE SAME THING over and over?

The koala certainly doesn't; adult koalas eat nothing but leaves from the eucalyptus tree. So it's not the taste that wears them out. Eucalyptus is so difficult to digest, koalas must take it easy in order to save enough energy to digest their leafy lunch. As a result, they can spend 20 hours a day sleeping, preferring to come out at night when it is safer to be so slow. While sleeping all day on a branch might make your backside sore, koalas have it covered: Fur on their bottoms grows extra-thick to prepare them for a life of tree lounging.

Brown Bear

During the winter, there's a good chance brown bears are sleeping at the same time as you are; but they are probably sleeping **WHILE YOU ARE AWAKE,** too. These supersleepers will nap for up to 6 months during their winter hibernation, if left undisturbed. Unlike other animals, which set their sleep schedules to avoid being eaten by larger predators, the brown bear is bigger than most—it grows nearly 10 feet (3 meters) long and weighs up to 1,500 pounds (680 kilograms). Its biggest threat is its hunger; it eats up to 90 pounds (40 kilograms) a day! So, it sleeps during the winter when food is scarce.

Giant Pacific Octopus

If this octopus lived on land, it'd probably spend most of its time **IN THE SHADE.** Underwater, the giant Pacific octopus spends as much time in darkness as it can. Waiting until night to hunt fish, clams, sharks, and even birds, it takes whatever it grabs with its 6-feet-long (2-meter-long) arms back to its dark den to eat. Drilling for dinner with its salivary papilla (a teeth-covered organ), an octopus can crack the toughest shells. When threatened, it has several tricks up its sleeves: It can squirt black ink to mask its getaway, detach *and* regenerate its arms, or change colors for camouflage.

Beaver

Know anyone who SNORES SO LOUDLY it sounds like they're sawing logs? Beavers really do spend all night cutting trees, but they don't use saws; they use their two front teeth. Beavers are so busy at night, they probably do more while you're sleeping than you do all day. In 1 week, a group of beavers can cut down trees and construct a dam 30 feet (9 meters) long. But how do beavers keep their teeth from wearing out? The teeth just keep growing. Beavers are constantly wearing down their teeth, which keeps them from getting too long.

Zzzzz Pangolin

Are pangolins PERFECT for picnics?

They don't mind if ants show up. At pangolin picnics, ants wouldn't be pests; they'd be the meal. With no teeth and a long, sticky tongue, about all these scaly animals can eat are ants and termites. There'd always be a ball to play with: Pangolins roll up into balls for defense. Once rolled up, they can even roll away. Why aren't pangolins invited to every picnic? They spray a powerfully stinky spray when upset and they come out only at night. Females spend 3-4 hours every night foraging for food and males spend at least twice as long. Unless you like your picnics dark and smelly, better not bother inviting a pangolin.

Grunion

Going on **A GRUNION RUN** can be a lot of fun . . . as long as you go on the right night. The grunion fish comes out on only specific nights, but those who are familiar with the cycle of ocean tides can predict when they will appear. When grunions do decide it's time to "run," they can be some of the easiest fish to catch. Technically, they don't have legs, so they don't really run, but they truly are fish out of water. When the night tides are just right, for a few hours, they ride waves onto the beaches of Southern California by the thousands, to spawn and lay their eggs in the sand.

Z Z Z Z Z River Otter

Ever been told it's late and YOU "OTTER" GO TO BED? River otters get told a lot of things when they're young; rather, they're taught a lot of things. Since otters hunt at night, baby otters learn to go to bed early in the morning. Their mothers must also teach them how to swim and catch fish. Otter moms will catch fish and release them so their pups can practice fishing for themselves. Luckily for otters, their learning looks like a lot of fun. It's not uncommon to see otters goofing around, swishing down slides of mud or snow. These "games" help teach otters how to survive in their environment.

Raccoon

If you've ever been woken up in the middle of the night by a CRASHING TRASH CAN, there's a good chance it was a raccoon looking for dinner. Raccoons' habitat is no longer restricted to rural areas. Thanks to their stubbornness when it comes to traveling far and their willingness to eat anything, raccoons live just about everywhere—from forests to marshes to prairies, and now cities. If they're awake all night, where do they sleep all day? They prefer to nest high up in tree hollows, but they have no problem calling a house's attic home.

ZZZZZ Puma

How do you eat a porcupine? VERY CAREFULLY . . . unless you're a puma, in which case, you gobble it up whole.

Eating porcupines isn't the only "trick" these cats do for a treat. Because they're able to jump 18 feet (5.5 meters) straight up from the ground, it's no wonder these athletic cats have a shoe named after them. Unfortunately for their prey, they're just as skilled at jumping out of trees as they are at jumping into them. Using their stealth to stalk their prey, pumas are known as ambush hunters. This is why they come out primarily at night instead of during the day, with dusk and dawn being their prime feeding times.

Hippopotamus

When you weigh over 9,000 pounds (4,080 kilograms), you get to **CHOOSE YOUR OWN BEDTIME.** The hippopotami have decided to spend up to 18 hours a day sleeping or resting just below the surfaces of lakes and rivers. Why not? No animal in Africa scares them, so they don't have to wait until night to crawl out of their watery hangouts. Why wait until dark to eat their nightly meals of more than 80 pounds (36 kilograms) of grass? They have sensitive skin. Even though their bodies secrete their own sunblock, hippos need to stay in the water to keep from getting sunburned or from dehydrating.

ZZ_ZZ_Z Wild Boar

Have you ever been SO BORED, you fell asleep?

Wild boars must know how you feel, because they'll often spend 12 hours during the day resting in the shade. When they do get up at night, it's to look for food. They spend the 4–8 hours a night foraging for fruit, nuts, insects, eggs, dead animals, trash . . . they're pigs; they'll eat almost anything! But it must not be too exciting, because wild boars will usually take at least one nap before the night is over. When they're not resting, they partake in one of their favorite activities, wallowing: rolling around in mud or water to protect themselves from the sun and insects.

Boa Constrictor

When BATS ARE YOUR FAVORITE MEAL, you better like the nightlife. As it happens, boa constrictors have no issue hanging out once the sun goes down. How do big boas nab nimble bats? By dangling from branches near cave openings. When bats take their nightly flight, boas bite them right out of the air. When not bobbing for bats, boas hunt for a variety of other prey, from rats to wild pigs, by using special heat-sensing scales. But what the boa eats isn't the most unbelievable thing about it. Perhaps the freakiest thing a boa does is give birth—up to 60 live boa babies, each one up to 2 feet (0.6 meter) long!

Z Z Z Z Z

Japanese Giant Salamander

Just because it spends all day SLEEPING UNDER A ROCK doesn't mean the Japanese giant salamander is clueless. This 6-feet-long (1.8-meter-long) monster is crafty enough to live for well over 50 years, even though it is nearly blind and unable to hear. What's its secret? It has several. It hunts at night, when its poor eyesight isn't a problem. Its body is also highly sensitive to changes in the water. When it senses a change, it snaps its large mouth to feast on fish, crabs, insects, and mice. It can even go weeks without eating, if needed. When threatened, it secretes a slimy substance that smells like Japanese peppers to help ward off would-be predators.

Camel Spider

With its scientific name *Solifugae* meaning **"FLEEING FROM THE SUN,"** it's no wonder the camel spider prefers the nighttime over the day. Something that isn't small on this arachnid are its jaws. Nearly one-third the size of the rest of its body, they are the largest jaws (relative to body size) on the planet. The enormous jaws certainly make camel spiders scary, but that's the point. Since camel spiders aren't poisonous, they use their gigantic jaws, along with lightning-quick speed, to capture and tear apart late-night prey, such as other spiders, scorpions, rodents, and small birds.

Moon Migration

It probably comes as NO SURPRISE that some species of owls migrate during the evening hours.

But they're not alone in their moonlit migrations. More than a dozen different birds, including thrashers, creepers, blackbirds, orioles, sparrows, and bobolinks, take flight at night when it's time to follow their preferred seasons north or south. While bird-watchers use the light of full moons to help them observe these midnight migrations, it's believed the birds use stars to help them navigate, focusing on constellations such as the Big and Little Dippers as guides.

Vampire Flying Frog

Even though it gets darker outside at night, YOU STAY THE SAME COLOR DURING THE NIGHT that you are during the day. But this isn't true for every animal in nature. Scientists have recently discovered a new species of frog in the cloud forests—forests so humid, there is always fog around them—of southern Vietnam. The vampire flying frog changes from a dull tan in the day to a bright red during the night. The *flying* part of its name comes from the way its webbed feet spread out and allow it to glide from tree to tree. The *vampire* comes from the two fangs it has when it's a tadpole. Scientists still aren't sure what purpose they serve, but they're the first fangs ever seen on tadpoles.

NATURE:
No Time for
NAPPING

Z
Z
Z
Z
Z

Moonflower

Believe it or not, plants don't have flowers to make you **OOH** and **AH**. They have flowers to attract insects to help them pollinate and make more plants. Since there are so many plants that need to pollinate during the day, some plants, like the moonflower, would rather let all of the busy bees be and attract a different set of insects: moths. If you've seen moths at night, you know how much they like light; so does the moonflower. With bright white petals that bloom only at night, this flower is flocked by moths before the sun comes up and its petals die and disappear.

Giant Hogweed

If you ever rub up against the giant hogweed, staying up at night and sleeping during the day—along with staying away from sunlight—is one of the only ways to **PROTECT YOURSELF.** Growing as tall as 15 feet (4.6 meters) and with leaves as broad as 5 feet (1.5 meters), it's no wonder how it got the *giant* in its name. But perhaps *giant vampire weed* would be a more fitting name. If any of its clear sap gets on your skin, you probably won't even know it . . . until you walk into sunlight. When UV rays from the sun hit the toxins in the sap, the sap burns and blisters the skin and can even cause blindness, if it gets in your eyes.

Zzzz Mount Everest

Do you EVER DREAM of climbing Everest? If so, the longer you wait to summit the world's tallest mountain, the higher you'll have to go. This massive mountain has been growing for over tens of millions of years, and it hasn't stopped. Every night you're asleep, Mount Everest is adding another 0.007 inches (0.02 centimeters) to its 29,035 feet (8,850 meters). While scientists can agree how "fast" this giant is growing, two nations are in disagreement as to how it should be measured. China believes Everest should be measured from its base to its last rock on top; Nepal thinks it should be measured to the height of its snow—a difference of about 13 feet (4 meters).

Hot Spring

A warm bath before bed can help you fall asleep. Well, there's a **WARM BATH** and there's a **HOT BATH.** While North Americans are climbing into bed at night, on the other side of the planet in New Zealand, tourists are visiting the world's largest hot spring. The appropriately named Frying Pan Lake is about 409,029 square feet (38,000 square meters) and filled with water so hot—113°-131°F (45°-55°C)—that you can hear it sizzling as if it's frying bacon. The lake fills a crater created by the Tarawera volcano when it "woke up" with an eruption in 1886. A second eruption in 1917 cracked the earth again, releasing underground water to fill the crater.

NATURE

Zzzzz Jet Stream

I SCREAM, you SCREAM, we all SCREAM for . . . the jet stream? It may not be as sweet as ice cream, but the jet stream is just as cool. Floating 4-9 miles (6-14 kilometers) up in the sky, this stream helps jets fly faster and drives weather systems from west to east across the globe. This gush of high-altitude air reaches average speeds of 55 or 100 miles per hour (90 or 160 kilometers per hour), depending on if it is summer or winter, and can travel as fast as 275 miles per hour (442 kilometers per hour). That means while you're sleeping, this large river of air can push a weather system an average of 800 miles (1,287 kilometers) in the wintertime. That's as far as San Francisco, California, to Seattle, Washington.

NATURE

Old Faithful

As it turns out, Old Faithful ISN'T THAT FAITHFUL. Contrary to popular belief, Yellowstone's most popular geyser doesn't erupt every hour on the hour. But you can count on its blowing its top every 35–20 minutes. And this geyser never sleeps. It sprays water from its spout day and night. Since it averages 21–23 eruptions per day, it's a pretty safe bet that around eight or so are happening while you're asleep. Recently, scientists have been learning a lot about Yellowstone's geysers. Not only do they believe the amount of rainfall in the park affects the frequency of geyser eruptions, they also now speculate the hot water underneath Old Faithful is powerful enough to supply energy to 30,000 homes.

NATURE

Z Z Z Z Z

Sky Glow

What is sky glow? It **SOUNDS A LOT COOLER THAN IT IS,** and if you happen to be an astronomer or amateur stargazer, it's one of your biggest enemies. For most people, though, sky glow isn't noticed because it occurs primarily while they're asleep. Sky glow is the wide-ranging light given off by cities into the night sky. This is why it appears that there are more stars in a country sky than in a city sky: there is the same number of stars, just a different level of sky glow. The sky glow of a major city can be so powerfully bright, it can interfere with one's view of the night sky as far as 200 miles (322 kilometers) away from the city center.

Underwater Light Show

While you sleep your summer nights away, **SOMETHING FREAKY HAPPENS** in the waters along Florida's space coast. For a few weeks each summer, it appears as if stars have fallen into the waters along this coast. But they're not stars that are twinkling below the surface, they're bioluminescent microorganisms (tiny, glowing organisms). Just like fireflies, these organisms give off light to communicate with one another. Some of them even respond directly to movement in the water. If the water is too dark, just dip in your hand and watch them glow. It might be worth sleeping through the sunshine for one day so you can spend an evening swimming with the stars.

Z Z Z Z Z

The Bat Plant

Ever hear of a NOISY PLANT?

The Cuban plant known as *Marcgravia evenia* doesn't exactly make any noises of its own, but the shape of its leaves—curved like satellite dishes—creates an extra-loud target for bats. Most plants have brightly colored flowers to attract daytime fliers to help them pollinate other plants. But bright colors are not much use in the dark of night when bats are about. The special shape of the *M. evenia* leaves appeals to the bats, which rely on echolocation for navigating the night. Echolocation is the process of sending out tiny pulses of sound that bounce back whenever they hit objects, allowing bats to sense their surroundings. The bats then help pollinate these responsive plants.

Rainfall

For many, the **SOUND OF RAIN** helps them go to sleep. Does that mean it rains more at night than during the day? Nope. The time of day doesn't determine when it rains. Rainfall is caused by a complex system involving temperature, evaporation, and air pressure. But during the monsoon season of Cherrapunji, India, it might seem as if it never stops raining. Cherrapunji holds the world record for the highest annual rainfall: From August 1860 to July 1861, it received 87 feet (26.5 meters) of rain. On average, it receives 36 feet (11 meters) of rain a year, making it one of the wettest places on Earth—night or day.

NATURE

Z Z Z Z Moon Bow

What could be MORE EXCITING than a double rainbow?

How about a moon bow? What's a moon bow? It is the extremely rare rainbow that occurs only at night. Most rainbows seen during the day are caused by bright light reflecting off water drops. The ingredients for a moon bow are a little more complicated, since moonlight is thousands of times less bright than sunlight. What's needed: the moon resting at no more than 42 degrees' height in a pitch-black sky and rain falling across the moon. It's yet to be determined whether or not pots of gold can be found at the end of moon bows.

NATURE

Earth Cooling

Your body isn't the ONLY THING THAT COOLS OFF when it goes to sleep at night. The Earth cools off at night as well. And it's a good thing it does. Since heat is cumulative—it builds, little by little—if the Earth never cooled off, we'd all burn up. This is why the hottest time of the day is in the afternoon, when the sun is already going down—instead of noon, when it is at its brightest. The same is true when it comes to cooling down; the Earth is at its coolest early in the morning, just before you—and the sun—get up.

NATURE

Zzzzz Coral Reef

Some organisms NEVER STOP GROWING ... or building, in the case of coral.

Technically, coral reefs never sleep, so while you're fast asleep, millions of tiny organisms—both plant and animal—are slow at work, adding to the coral reefs of the Earth's oceans. Even though billions of different organisms participate in creating a coral reef, its basic structure is primarily built by organisms called polyps. From a distance, during the day, polyps might appear to be peaceful plants or colorful rocks; however, at night, they'll toss out their sharp, venomous tentacles to grab zooplankton or fish for a late-night snack.

NATURE

Mount Saint Helens

The evening of May 17, 1980, was the **LAST NIGHT OF SLEEP** for 57 people and thousands of plants and animals surrounding Mount Saint Helens. At 8:32 a.m., on May 18, the mountain blew its top, resulting in the most devastating volcanic eruption in U.S. history. Luckily, scientists studying the volcano had been giving warnings for months leading up to the explosion. As a result, residents who lived around the mountain had plenty of notice to get away. Even though an estimated 7,000 large animals perished, the number could have been much higher. Many of the nocturnal animals that lived around the mountain had already gone to sleep by the time the volcano exploded, hidden in shelters or underground burrows.

NATURE

ZZZZ Dead Sea Dying

The Dead Sea, surrounded by Jordan, Israel, and Palestine, isn't just dead, IT'S DYING. The *dead* in its name comes from the fact that it is so saturated with salt, hardly anything can live in it; only the tiniest forms of bacteria and algae have been able to call it home. It's not really a sea, either; it's a salt *lake.* Every year, roughly 55 inches (140 centimeters) of its water evaporates—that's about 0.15 inches (3.8 millimeters) total at the end of each day. If it keeps drying up at this rate, though, it could have its name for an entirely different reason: It might cease to exist!

Blue Waves

Few things are as sleep inducing as the WAVES CRASHING ON A BEACH at night. But if those waves rolling in are glowing a neon blue, they can be just plain creepy. If you're ever in San Diego, California, in late August and see some neon waves crashing at night, don't worry; it's not an underwater uprising of glowing, toxic aquatic organisms . . . wait, actually, it is. The scientific name of this slightly toxic algae is *Lingulodinium polyedrum*, but locals call it red tide. Why the color-changing name? This algae is really a dull brown color, causing waters to appear rusty during the day. However, when a large amount of the algae moves together, it creates a chemical reaction that sends off flashes of light. These blue flashes can be seen only in the darkness of night.

NATURE

Zzzz Mississippi Moving

Want to hear a BEDTIME STORY? Then take a trip down the Mississippi River. Mark Twain once described the river as a "wonderful book with a new story to tell every day." Until you take that trip, here's something to dream about: A raindrop that falls into Lake Itasca, in northern Minnesota (where the Mississippi River begins), will take about 90 days to reach the river's end at the Gulf of Mexico. That means every night you're asleep, this drop of rain is floating an average of 26 miles (42 kilometers) down the mighty Mississippi.

NATURE

Wildfires

Unfortunately, **WILDFIRES DON'T ONLY OCCUR IN NIGHTMARES.** They can start and spread anytime, day or night. However, nighttime can be a wildfire fighter's best friend. When the night comes, three things typically happen: There's more humidity, wind slows down, and cooler air settles in. All of these things can be huge helps in keeping a fire from spreading. Advances in technology have also made fighting fires much safer and more effective. Up until the mid-1940s, around 20 million acres (8 million hectares) of forest would burn in the United States every year. Today, only about 4 million acres (1.6 million hectares) are lost to forest fires. That's a drop from an average of 54,795 acres (22,175 hectares) a day to 10,959 acres (4,435 hectares).

NATURE

Desert Stones Sailing

Zzzz

Stones SAIL ACROSS THE DESERT as you sleep. No, it's not the stuff of dreams or pranks played by aliens. In a section of Death Valley, in California, stones weighing up to 700 pounds (318 kilograms) have been mysteriously moving across the desert, leaving trails hundreds of feet long in the dry desert surface. Since they weigh too much to have been moved by strong winds, and no earthquakes coincide with their movements, these rocky travelers have puzzled scientists for decades. Recently, though, scientists have developed a theory: At night, water in the top layer of soil freezes, creating an "ice collar" around the stones. Then, as the weather warms a month later, the ice melts and the stones sail away, floating on the water from the melted ice.

Icebergs Floating

At 20 minutes after midnight on April 15, 1912, **OVER 2,000 PEOPLE ON BOARD** the *Titanic* were awoken. What woke them? An iceberg. While most of the ship was asleep, the *Titanic* tried to navigate its way through a field of floating ice. What those awake did see was an iceberg now believed to have been around 50-100 feet (15-30 meters) high and 200-400 feet (61-123 meters) long. What they didn't see was the other 90 percent of it below the surface of the water. Every year, about 15,000 icebergs are formed and float off from Arctic glaciers. That means, on average, 41 new icebergs plop into the northern seas every night!

ZZZZZ

The World's Most Active Mountain at Night

Every night on the summit of Hawaii's highest point, Mauna Kea, a collection of the **MOST POWERFUL TELESCOPES IN THE WORLD** go into action. With 13 telescopes, and astronomers from 11 different countries operating them to study the universe, Mauna Kea is the largest astronomical observatory on the planet. But astronomers didn't choose Mauna Kea so they could live near tropical beaches; they did so because it's 13,796 feet (4,205 meters) above sea level, and that keeps them above the humidity and air pollution. Not only are the skies clear, but they're as dark as possible. Since Mauna Kea is so far away from the nearest city, there are no lights to interfere with the telescopes' views of the stars.

Ground Shaking While You're Sleeping

What could be a WORSE WAY TO WAKE UP from deep sleep than to an earthquake? Scary, but it happens. Since there are no specific seasons or times of day that earthquakes occur, it's best to always be prepared. According to the Federal Emergency Management Agency, if you're inside a house when an earthquake strikes, your bed is one of the safest places to be. Just make sure you're not close to any windows, and cover your head with a pillow. Where's the safest place to be during an earthquake? Outside—away from any buildings or utility poles. That's right, no need to worry about the ground opening up and swallowing you whole, that only happens in movies . . . and nightmares.

NATURE

ZZ
ZZ
Z

One Grand Party

Approximately 13,000 people visit the Grand Canyon every day, making it one of the MOST-VISITED ATTRACTIONS in the United States. As awe inspiring as it might appear during the day, most people leave before they can enjoy its nighttime beauty. However, for those who forsake their sleep and stick around for the stars to come out, there are views of the universe that cannot be seen from anywhere else on the planet. Part of the secret behind such splendid sights of the stars is that there are no lights from buildings, streets, or signs to interfere. Every June since 1991, amateur and professional astronomers have been gathering at the Grand Canyon to stay up all night stargazing at the annual Grand Canyon Star Party.

Antarctic Ice Freezing and Melting

Even while you're sleeping, the Antarctic ice sheet is **BUSY EITHER MELTING OR REFREEZING.** In fact, during the winter, 6,000 square miles (15,500 square kilometers) of the continent's surrounding seawater freeze every night. That's approximately 67 square miles (173 square kilometers) every day. By the time winter is over, the continent of Antarctica will have frozen enough ice to nearly double its size. Then, during the summer months, it all melts again. In total, the amount of seawater around Antarctica that melts and refreezes is about three times the size of the United States.

NATURE

ZZZZZ

One Very Sensitive Plant

Have you ever felt so shy, you wanted to HIDE SO NO ONE COULD SEE or bother you?

You're not alone. Every night, as you're tucking in, the *Mimosa pudica* is folding up. This plant is so sensitive, even the slightest touch against its leaves causes it to fold up and then drop down. Even when untouched, the leaves of this plant respond to changes in the day. When the sun goes down, the plant goes to sleep by folding up its leaves and letting its branches droop. When the morning comes, the leaves open back up for the rest of the day, to soak in the sun. Scientists aren't sure why the plant is so sensitive and, apparently, scared of the dark, but they suspect its sensitivity may protect it from leaf-eating insects.

Four Presidents Who Never Sleep

Even though their terms are long over, Presidents George Washington, Thomas Jefferson, Theodore Roosevelt, and Abraham Lincoln remain **WIDE AWAKE ON THE SIDE OF MOUNT RUSHMORE.** It's doubtful, though, that anyone got much sleep during the 14 years it took artist Gutzon Borglum to complete the sculpture—90 percent of the sculpture was carved out of the mountainside using dynamite. Rain, wind, snow, and wedges of ice forming in cracks are all slowly chipping away at the surface of the sculpture. Don't worry; you still have plenty of time to see the presidents. The rate of erosion is about 1 inch (2.5 centimeters) every 10,000 years.

NATURE

ZZ Z Z Z

Ring around the Moon Means Rain Soon

Have you ever STARED AT THE MOON and wondered what the rings around it were?

No, the moon is no angel, but it can have a halo. Known as a lunar halo, these rings aren't even around the moon. In fact, they're much closer to us than the moon is. The rings we see are actually moonlight bouncing off ice crystals in cirrus clouds floating about 20,000 feet (6,100 meters) above the Earth's surface. Since high cirrus clouds often bring storms, rings can be an indication that rain is on the way.

Glaciers Sliding

For most, just the thought of WATCHING A GLACIER MOVE would be sleep inducing.

However, many glaciers today are starting to pick up their pace. Some of the fastest glaciers on Earth can be found in and around Alaska, where they are moving about 50 feet (15 meters) a night while you're asleep. So, for an entire day, they move 150 feet (46 meters). That's almost as long as an Olympic-size swimming pool! Where are these melting glaciers going? Most are sliding down mountains. The rocky surface acts as speed bumps, keeping these glaciers moving slowly enough to stop from crashing into pipelines, people, and towns at the bottoms of mountains.

NATURE

ZzZzz

Earth's Surface Never Sleeps

Believe it or not, you don't WAKE UP IN THE SAME PLACE as you went to sleep. How's that possible? The Earth is constantly moving—and not just spinning around as it circles the sun. The Earth's surface is moving every night you're asleep. Not that you'll be able to tell that you woke up in a different spot than where you fell asleep. The Earth's surface might constantly be in motion, but that doesn't mean it's in any hurry. During one evening of sleep, the ground moves only about 0.0007-0.004 inch (0.002-0.009 centimeter). Who knows, if it moved any farther, it might wake you up!

Sleeping Through a Storm

z z z z Z Z

It might seem **TERRIFYING TO TRY TO SLEEP** while lightning flashes all around you outside, but your bed is one of the safest places you can be during a thunderstorm . . . unless you're using your home phone. Talking on the phone during a thunderstorm is the number-one cause of in-home lightning injuries. How many bolts of lightning are you avoiding? On average, the Earth will be struck by lightning nearly 3 million times during the night. Better pull up your covers . . . and hang up your phone!

Zzzzz An Up-and-Down Night

You'd probably never even notice unless you FELL ASLEEP ON A BEACH, but tides (the ocean's water level) move up and down during the night. What causes this change? The sun and the moon both affect tides, but the moon has a greater impact, since it is much closer. The moon is big enough and close enough for its gravitational pull to actually draw the Earth's water toward it as it passes by. Because of this, the Earth experiences two high tides and two low tides every lunar day, which is how long it takes the moon to circle the Earth: 24 hours, 50 minutes. So, the ocean closest to you will rise up to its high tide *and* fall back to its low tide all before you wake up in the morning.

Amazon at Night

Z Z Z Z Z

Have you ever woken up from a deep sleep, only to discover you've been sleeping in **A POOL OF DROOL?** No matter how much spit leaked out of your mouth, it's nothing compared to the amount of water the Amazon River unleashes every night while you're asleep. With a river winding about 4,195 miles (6,752 kilometers) long, the Amazon empties just under 3 *trillion* gallons (10 trillion liters) of water into the Atlantic Ocean every night. Don't feel bad, though; the mouth of the Amazon River is a bit larger than yours—it's over 250 miles (400 kilometers) wide!

NATURE

ZZZZ World's Biggest Waterfall

Some things in nature NEVER SLEEP.

Take Victoria Falls (or Mosi-oa-Tunya, as it is known by locals), which rushes over the border of Zambia and Zimbabwe. Stretching 1.25 miles (2 kilometers) wide and up to 354 feet (108 meters) high, it keeps the waters from the Zambezi River flowing night and day. So much water goes over its edge that, during an evening's sleep in February and March (when water volume is at its highest), up to 9 trillion cubic feet (259 billion cubic meters) of water will wash over. That's like watching 45 *trillion* soccer balls tumble over the falls in a single night!

Night-Blooming Orchid

NEW AND REMARKABLE DISCOVERIES are constantly being made, even at night.

In November 2011, scientists discovered a new species of orchid they've named *Bulbophyllum nocturnum*. What makes this orchid stand apart from the other 2,000 species is that it's the only one to flower solely at night. All the other orchids aren't as picky: They flower during the night *and* day. Not only does this flower come out exclusively at night, it comes out for one night of the year only. It's still too early for scientists to know why the flower makes such a limited appearance, but they will be working day and night to learn the reason.

NATURE

Zzzz One Prickly Night

If you come out only one night a year, you might as well MAKE IT SPECTACULAR. That's exactly what the night-blooming cereus does. Ordinarily, this cactus isn't much to look at. But, for one special night, it's worth staying up for. At around 9 or 10 p.m. that evening, its buds will break open and white, waxy, trumpet-shaped flowers, 14 inches (35 centimeters) long and 9 inches (23 centimeters) wide, will bloom before your eyes. By midnight, they'll be in full bloom. But, by the time the sun comes back up, its flowers will wither away.

When the Desert Freezes Over

After extra water, what would be the FIRST THING YOU'D PACK to spend a night in the desert?

You might want to pack an air conditioner, but you'd be better off packing an extra blanket. Although deserts do get very hot during the day, at night, they cool off considerably. In some cases, temperatures drop to about 40°F (4°C). Sometimes, desert temperatures even drop below freezing, that is, below 32°F (0°C). This rapid change in temperature is caused by what deserts lack below and above: water. With little water below the surface, it doesn't take long for the surface to heat up during the day, and cloudless skies allow the heat, built up from the day, to escape at night.

NATURE

ZZZZz

Uneasy Underwater

Things might look peaceful underwater, but deep below the sea, **THINGS ARE HARDLY AS SERENE AS THEY SEEM.** While you're sleeping so your body can grow, seafloors are changing and new islands are forming, as a result of undersea volcanoes. Nearly three-quarters of all volcanic eruptions happen below the surface of the world's oceans. At a depth of 3,900 feet (1,200 meters), the deepest submarine volcano we know about is West Mata, near the Fiji Islands. Its eruptions produce 3-feet-wide (1-meter-wide) gas-filled bubbles of lava that glow like giant lightbulbs. Considering how dark it is that far down in the ocean, they could be called nature's night-lights.

z Z Z Z

Inflating Volcano

One of the best parts about going to sleep is that it gives you a chance to UNWIND AND LET GO of some of the pressure built up from the day. Unfortunately for the volcano Uturuncu in Bolivia, its pressure is only growing. The hot magma coming from below the surface of the Earth is filling it up as if it's a balloon being filled with air. During one night's sleep, the 20,000-feet-tall (6,000-meter-tall) volcano will be supplied with 777,600 cubic feet (22,019 cubic meters) more magma. That's 10 times faster than the inflation of a typical volcano. But there's no need to lose any sleep over its eruption; scientists don't believe it will blow its top anytime soon.

NATURE

ZZZZZ

Bamboo's Big Night

Is the thought of WATCHING GRASS GROW enough to make you sleepy?

That should depend on the type of grass you're watching. The fastest-growing bamboo on record can grow up to 4 feet (1.2 meters) in a day. So, when you wake up in the morning, this bamboo will be more than 12 inches (30 centimeters) taller than it was when you went to bed. Not only is this grass fast, it's versatile. People use bamboo to build everything from suspension bridges to beds.

Millennium Seed Bank

With every passing night, there are nearly 100,000 plants growing **CLOSER TO EXTINCTION.** But, if scientists working at the Millennium Seed Bank have their way, plant lovers should be able to rest easier. Instead of holding money safely in its highly secured vaults, this bank is storing thousands of seeds underground. The seeds are dried, cleaned, put into special containers, and then kept at a frigid -4°F (-20°C). They must be stored this way to keep them fresh so, if a species of plant ever goes extinct in the wild, seeds from the bank can be used to reintroduce it. Remarkably, even though the Millennium Seed Bank has seeds to more than 24,000 different species of plants, this represents only about 10 percent of all plant species on Earth.

NATURE

Zzzz Saturn's Day

If you slept 10 hours and 14 seconds each night, that would equal ONE DAY on SATURN.

You could go to sleep just as the sun was going down on Saturn and by the time you woke up, the sun would be going down again! There's another problem, if you actually tried to spend a day on Saturn—you wouldn't be able to stand. Saturn is a gas giant. That means it doesn't have a solid surface to hold you or your bed.

Halley's Comet

What careens across the sky up to **122,000 MILES PER HOUR** (196,380 kilometers per hour) and looks like a 9-mile-long (15-kilometer-long), 5-mile-wide (8 kilometer-wide) peanut? Stumped? Here's another clue: It can only be seen in the night sky every 76 years. It's Halley's comet. This galactic speedball is at its fastest when traveling near the sun, but slows down to a mere 2,000 miles per hour (3,276 kilometers per hour) when it is at its farthest distance from the sun, beyond the planet Neptune. So, at its fastest, it can cover nearly 1 million miles (1.6 million kilometers) during one night's sleep.

SPACE

Neptune's Nutty Weather

The winds on Neptune are so fast, during a single night's sleep they could cover a distance of 12,800 miles (20,600 kilometers), making them THE FASTEST WINDS in our solar system. Neptune also holds our solar system's title of coldest planet, with an average temperature of about -391°F (-235°C). But the gusting winds and frigid cold on this giant gas ball of a planet aren't even its greatest weather features. You'll need to bring along a sturdy umbrella if you ever visit Neptune, because scientists suspect it rains diamonds! The presence of methane gas and extreme pressure naturally form diamonds in its atmosphere that then rain down.

Good-Bye, Moon

When you **STARE UP AT THE MOON** as you lie down at night, you might as well say good-bye in addition to good night. Don't worry, it won't be the last time you see it, but as you're drifting off to sleep, the moon is slowly drifting away. Every year, the moon moves another 1.5 inches (3.8 centimeters) away from the Earth. That means every night while you are sleeping, it creeps another 0.001 inch (0.003 centimeter) off into space. Why is it sneaking away? Because it's a thief! As it orbits the Earth, it "steals" some of the Earth's rotational energy; it then uses this "stolen" energy to increase the size and distance of its own orbit.

Moon Myths

Does a full moon at night mean **YOU SHOULD BE MORE WORRIED** about your safety?

It may be hard to believe, but long ago, some people thought that werewolves came out to hunt on these special nights. Even today, some people believe that crime, emergency room visits, and surgeon slipups are increased during full moons. However, scientists have done their best to howl at these myths by performing studies. Each study has proven that the moon has little effect on our behavior, only our beliefs. So, enjoy the moonlight and sleep soundly.

EMERGENCY ROOM

Earth's Sneaky Hitchhiker

In the summer of 2011, scientists announced that another large rock was **HITCHING A RIDE** on the Earth's solar orbit. It's a 1,000-feet-wide (300-meter-wide) asteroid called 2010 TK7. Earth isn't the only planet with this type of hitchhiker. Scientists refer to such asteroids as Trojans. Jupiter has over 5,000 of them! Why has it taken so long to spot Earth's first Trojan? Due to the path of its orbit, it can't be seen at night, and the brightness of the sun's rays had hidden it during the day. That is, until NASA launched its Wide-Field Infrared Survey Explorer (WISE) to stargaze during the day.

SPACE

Z Z Z Z Juno Jupiter?

Did you know that as you go to sleep every night, the GALAXY'S TINIEST SPACE CREW is traveling toward Jupiter?

On August 5, 2011, NASA launched its *Juno* spacecraft. There are no humans on board, but there are three Lego figurines to "man" the five-year flight. And these aren't just any random Lego figurines. Each has a connection to the giant gas ball Jupiter. Galileo Galilei, one of the most remarkable scientists to study Jupiter—and who discovered four of its moons—is on board, carrying a tiny telescope. The Roman god Jupiter, complete with lightning bolt, is going, since it *is* his planet, after all. And his wife, Juno, is going, carrying a magnifying glass as a symbol of the spacecraft's journey for truth about the planet.

SPACE

"GALILEO"   "JUNO"   "JUPITER"

Rosetta Spacecraft

Z Z Z Z Z

Bears MIGHT NOT HIBERNATE during June, but spacecraft apparently do.

On June 8, 2011, the *Rosetta* spacecraft went into hibernation. One of few things operating on the spacecraft during its hibernation will be its alarm clock to wake it up from its "deep sleep" on January 20, 2014. So, while you're sleeping, so is one of the most exciting spacecraft of our time. What's so exciting about it? When it wakes up, it's going to attempt to be the first spacecraft to land a vehicle on a comet. The person in charge of the project, Dr. Gerhard Schwehm, is so excited about *Rosetta*, he is quoted as saying about its waking: "I might not sleep the night before."

SPACE

Z Z Z Z Z *Dawn* Orbiter

Just as the **DAWN'S EARLY LIGHT** can be bright enough to wake up even the soundest sleeper, scientists are also hoping to "wake up" to many mysteries of how our solar system was formed, with data collected from the *Dawn* orbiter. As you're fast asleep—and while you're awake—*Dawn* is flying through an asteroid belt, studying the Vesta asteroid and the dwarf planet Ceres. Launched in 2007, it began its orbit around Vesta on July 16, 2011, and has since moved on to Ceres, where it will be for the next three years. When it was launched, it was only 7.8 feet (2.4 meters) long, but once in space, it extended its solar panels to become 65 feet (19.7 meters) long. That's like transforming from a motorcycle to a tractor trailer!

SPACE

Comets in Space

Z Z Z Z Z

Since comets such as Halley's and Hale-Bopp MAKE THE NEWS ONLY EVERY FEW DECADES, it's easy to think comets aren't all that common. However, every night, there are an estimated 1 trillion—that's right, *trillion* with 12 zeros—comets zooming around our solar system. They're not as big, bright, or old as all of those twinkling stars, and instead of being big balls of flames, comets are covered in ice: enough ice to circle the sun several hundred times. Where do comets come from? Many comets in our solar system fly out of the Oort Cloud, a large cloud of comets on the far edge of the solar system.

SPACE

...998,637,816...
...UM...UM... OH RATS!!
...1,2,3,4,5...

Zzzzz Star Wars Planet

SOMETIMES, SCIENCE FICTION BECOMES SCIENCE REALITY.

More than 30 years ago, scientists around the world laughed when they saw the planet Tatooine in the movie *Star Wars*. Ha! A planet with two suns? Impossible, most scientists agreed. But as of September 2011, you can go to sleep knowing in a galaxy far, far away (about 200 light-years), there is a real planet with two suns. The planet, named Kepler 16b, takes about 229 days to orbit around its pair of stars, each of which is smaller than the Earth's sun. So, when you go to bed, dream big. Who knows when your strangest dreams might someday turn out to be true!

Alien Solar System Under Attack

Z **Z** **Z** **Z** **Z**

Don't worry, you can sleep easy; it's not *our* solar system that's under attack, and IT'S NOT ALIENS doing the attacking. Scientists have discovered something freaky happening every night to a solar system much like our own. While you're safely asleep on planet Earth as it orbits our sun, in the planetary system surrounding the star Eta Corvi, storms of icy comets are slamming into planets every night. The Eta Corvi system is so far away, scientist can't actually see the comets colliding with the planets, or the planets themselves, but they can see the enormous band of dust that has been formed from what's left of the comets after they've been pulverized by their collisions. Scientists also believe our Earth went through a similar storm billions of years ago. Their theory is that the ice from these colliding comets is what brought water to our rocky planet.

SPACE

ZZZ_{ZZ} Halloween Fireballs

GHOSTS AND GOBLINS aren't the only things that come out on Halloween night. If it's a clear night and you can see through your mask, there's a good chance you'll spot a shooting star or seven. That's right, starting around Halloween and then tapering off around mid-November is one of the most active meteor showers of the year. The annual event's official name is the Taurid meteor shower and, technically, the flashes of lights streaking across the sky are neither shooting stars nor Halloween fireballs. Instead, they are meteors made up of broken-off chunks of the comet Encke. Depending on the year, stargazers can spot anywhere from 7 to 15 meteors an hour.

New Horizons

We all know that, as of August 2006, PLUTO IS NO LONGER A PLANET. However, what else do scientists know about this dwarf planet? As it turns out, not much. That's where the *New Horizons* spacecraft comes in. Every night, since 2006, it has been hurtling through space on a mission of more than 3 billion miles (4.8 billion kilometers) to reach Pluto by July 2015. Its mission is to learn as much as it can about Pluto's surface and atmosphere. Its passengers? Ralph, Alice, Rex, and LORRI; but they aren't whom you might think they are. Ralph is the name for *New Horizons*'s infrared imager. Alice is the name for the device used to analyze Pluto's atmosphere. Rex is an instrument meant to take the temperature of the atmosphere. And LORRI (Long Range Reconnaissance Imager) is a telescopic camera that will be used to map Pluto's surface.

SPACE

Z Z Z Z Z

Mars Lander

Ever GO TO SLEEP CURIOUS about whether or not there's life on Mars?

You're not alone. On November 26, 2011, NASA launched *Curiosity*, as a part of its Mars Science Laboratory (MSL) mission to explore whether or not Mars has ever been capable of having life on it. This flying space lab rocketed through space until August 2012, when *Curiosity* finally landed on the surface of Mars to begin its exploration. In this case, "curiosity" is much more than a simple impulse: It's a 1-ton (0.9-metric-ton), nuclear-powered, six-wheeled, rolling robot, complete with a robotic arm and a laser capable of vaporizing Martian rocks up to 30 feet (9 meters) away. It doesn't hate rocks. Instead, the laser works with *Curiosity*'s ChemCam, a camera that can analyze the chemical makeup of vaporized rock particles.

SETI, Searching the Sky for Aliens

Have you ever stared at the stars and WONDERED IF there's anyone out there? Every night, after you stop wondering, some people are actually asking. Scientists working for the Search for Extraterrestrial Intelligence (SETI) Institute are constantly listening for radio signals in space, in attempts to detect the presence of other intelligent life-forms. So far, they haven't heard a call. However, the scientists at SETI are continuously working on refining the techniques they use to receive signals as well as focusing on the areas of space to which they are listening. We may never learn, within our lifetimes, whether or not we're alone in the universe.

Salt-Sniffing Satellites

It may be a **GOOD IDEA** to take a shower before you go to bed. With enough power to perceive a pinch of salt in a bucket of water from over 400 miles (644 kilometers) away in the sky, NASA's satellite *Aquarius* is studying our oceans, one "sniff" at a time. Rather than using a nose to detect the amount of salt present in the water, the satellite is using a selection of sophisticated sensors that can "sniff" the surface to collect its data. Through greater knowledge of the increases and decreases of salt content in ocean waters, scientists hope to better understand the causes and effects of climate change. Until then you might want to just make sure you change your socks before going to sleep—there's something sniffing in the sky.

Traveling Light

Z Z Z Z Z

Ever wonder **WHERE THE SUNLIGHT GOES** when you go to bed?

Light isn't stagnant; it's moving. In fact, the light you see from the sun took a little over 8 minutes to reach your eyes. So, if the sun ever shut off, it would take 8 minutes before you even knew it. But where does it go after it passes you by? To Pluto and beyond! If you watch a sunset at 9 p.m. and then go to sleep, that same light you saw is still traveling through space. In fact, at around 2:10 a.m. it will reach Pluto. By the time you wake up in the morning, the light will be streaking for another solar system.

SPACE

Hunting for Killer Asteroids

Zzzzz

Don't worry, you don't have to go to sleep wondering if THE SKY IS FALLING. However, you could worry a little about an asteroid falling out of the sky and striking the Earth. So far, out of the many asteroids in Earth's general orbit that scientists consider to be large enough to cause catastrophic damage to the Earth (i.e., asteroids over 460 feet [40 meters] wide), about only 15 percent have been tracked. Luckily, though, the biggest asteroid hunter on Earth was put into action in 2010. Located on the peak of Maui's Haleakala volcano, in Hawaii, is a new telescope that is also the world's largest digital camera. This camera, with its staggering 1,400 megapixels, takes over 500 photos every night in search of potential killer asteroids. By 2013, it is expected to examine 100,000 asteroids for possible danger, helping us all sleep a little easier.

SPACE

A Disturbance in the Oort

Where do some of the MOST DANGEROUS OBJECTS in the solar system come from?

No, not from Uranus, but from the Oort Cloud. The Oort Cloud is a huge collection of several billion comets orbiting around at the far edge of our solar system. Occasionally, comets from this cloud get knocked loose, causing them to "fall" toward our sun. This fall brings their orbits in closer to other planets in our solar system, including Earth. These disturbances in the Oort can occur at any time, even while you're sleeping. What makes comets potentially dangerous is the direction of their orbit in relationship with Earth: They may fly right at us! Unlike asteroids that trail Earth's orbit—which would cause a rear-end collision should they hit Earth—a comet fallen from Oort is more likely to be in a head-on collision.

SPACE

Zzzzz From Tenth to Dwarf

While you're asleep every night POWERFUL TELESCOPES are searching the sky for unknown objects. Astronomers in the Palomar Observatory take three pictures of one section of the night sky over a 3-hour period. Then they compare the pictures to look for any objects that moved. If something moves, it's likely an asteroid, comet, or sometimes, a new planet. In 2005, the discovery of an object in our solar system farther away from the sun and slightly larger than Pluto was announced. Scientists named this object Eris. At the time of its discovery, Pluto was still a planet, so Eris was to be the tenth planet in our solar system. Three years after Eris was discovered, Pluto was downgraded to a dwarf planet, taking Eris with it. Today, rather than being the 10th planet in our solar system, Eris is one of 44 known dwarf planets in it.

SPACE

YOU MUST BE THIS TALL

Earth Orbiting the Sun

z z z Z Z

You **DON'T MOVE** a whole lot while you're asleep, right?

Think again. If you're on planet Earth, you're moving; just as if you fall asleep in a car, you're still moving really fast, even if you don't *feel* like it. If a driver is obeying speed limits, you're probably not going to travel more than 70 miles per hour (113 kilometers per hour), but merely lying in bed blows those numbers away. The Earth is constantly traveling around the sun at a speed of 67,062 miles per hour (107,826 kilometers per hour)! How far do you travel every night while you're asleep? For every 8 hours you sleep at night, you're on a 536,496-mile (862,608-kilometer) journey.

SPACE

ZZZZ

Constellations Moving in the Night Sky

Constellations often depict creatures—**DOGS, DRAGONS, BULLS, AND HUNTERS**—and they appear in different parts of the sky, depending on when you look up at night. Does this mean these collections of stars are moving while you're sleeping? Yes, but not in the way you might think. The nightly journeys we see constellations make are not from their movements. Instead, they're from our movement. Stars appear to move from east to west across the sky because the Earth is spinning west to east. But this doesn't mean the stars in constellations are still. Since our galaxy is revolving around its center, the stars we see are all revolving, too. But they're so far away, it would take thousands of years for us to see any changes in their positions.

A Dusting of Mars

Z Z Z Z Z

What's **RED, SOLAR POWERED, AND TRAVELS UP TO 100 MILES PER HOUR** (161 kilometers per hour)—for a month at a time? No, it's not the latest "green" car, it's a Martian dust storm. While you're sound asleep, there's a good chance there's a dusty disturbance on Mars. These massive storms are created when the sun raises the planet's surface temperature; doing so causes winds to swirl; swirling winds pick up the dust covering Mars's surface. Once a storm starts, it can block out the sun for the entire planet in a matter of days for weeks at a time, making it appear to be nighttime all the time.

Z
Z
Z
Z
Z

Orion Hunting the Night Skies

Hunting is supposed to be a daytime activity, but NO ONE TOLD ORION that, because he's constantly stalking night skies. If you can see Orion, you can tell the time of year. For people in the northern hemisphere, Orion comes out in the winter; in the southern hemisphere, he appears during the summer. Thousands of years ago, people in the northern hemisphere looked to Orion for advice. If ancient peoples could find the mighty hunter, then so can you: Look for a line of three stars; this is his belt. The rest of his tunic is made up of two stars above his belt, and two below. If you're staring at a very clear sky, you should also be able to see his arms, holding his club in one hand and an unlucky lion in the other.

Moon Mapper

Every night since 2009, there's been A SPACECRAFT ORBITING THE MOON, taking **pictures of its surface.** The Lunar Reconnaissance Orbiter's (LRO) mission isn't to just snap some photos for a scrapbook; it's mapping the moon's surface in preparation for humans to return for future lunar exploration. In the time it's been circling the moon, it has collected enough data to fill more than 41,000 DVDs! With the power to spot objects as small as a picnic table, it's also exploring the far side of the moon. Previously, we knew much more about the moon's brightly lit near side. But the LRO has been bringing some fascinating facts to light about the far side of the moon, such as the South Pole-Aitken, one of the largest known impact basins in our solar system. Created by a collision with a comet or asteroid, this crater in the moon's surface is so deep, more than 34 Empire State Buildings could be stacked on top of one another in it. Now astronauts know one place *not* to land.

SPACE

ZZZZ Space Invaders

So far, Earth has never been **INVADED BY ALIENS.** But it has been invaded by objects from outer space before. It doesn't happen very often, but there have been cases of humans being attacked by alien objects. For one lucky person, Ann Hodges, it happened while she was sleeping. After lying down one day in 1954 to sleep, Hodges was woken up by getting hit in the hip by an 8-pound (3.6-kilogram) meteorite the size of a grapefruit. More recently, in 2009, a German teenager on his way to school was struck in the hand by a meteorite traveling more than 30,000 miles per hour (48,280 kilometers per hour). He survived, but the 3-inch (7.6-centimeter) scar on his hand probably makes him wish he had overslept for school that day.

SPACE

Worst Place to Fly a Kite

Venus has long been considered **EARTH'S TWIN**, due to its similar size and structure. Scientists are now studying another striking similarity between the two planets: lightning. In spite of huge differences in their atmospheres, both planets seem to be generating bolts of lightning of equal strength. If you ever plan on taking a kite to Venus, you should consider flying it at night, since Venus experiences fewer lightning strikes at night than during the day. And you better pack a lunch . . . and dinner—1 day on Venus is as long as 117 days on Earth, so the Venus equivalent of an 8-hour evening will last about 39 days!

SPACE

ZZZZZ Earth Spinning

Do you feel DIZZY when you wake up?

It's funny that you don't, because the Earth was spinning over 1,042 miles per hour (1,677 kilometers per hour) in a circle while you were asleep. So, if you get your 8 hours of sleep, you will also spin over 8,300 miles (13,400 kilometers) while you're dozing. Just how far will you "sleep travel"? If you were on an airplane instead of in your bed, you could travel from Los Angeles, California, to Bangkok, Thailand. No wonder you feel so tired when you wake up in the morning!

A Couple of Long-Range Voyagers

Every night, for more than 35 years, a pair of SPACE EXPLORERS has been researching the universe and sending back their findings to Earth. They are named *Voyager I* and *Voyager II*. Having completed their primary missions of studying Jupiter, Saturn, Uranus, and Neptune, the two explorers have now extended their exploration to the edge of our solar system. They have enough fuel to keep them flying until 2020 and then as far as the universe will take them. Thanks to these galactic travelers, we know more about the rings of Saturn, and that one of Jupiter's moons, Io, is covered with active volcanoes. Now there's something to dream about!

Zzzzz Eye in the Night Sky

As you're staring at the ceiling, waiting for sleep to come, the Hubble Telescope is orbiting the Earth at speeds of **5 MILES PER SECOND** (8 kilometers per second), and can pass the United States in about 10 minutes. When you wake up in the morning, it will have circled the Earth nearly five times. But it's not just going in circles, it's exploring the universe. With no clouds or pollution to get in the way, Hubble is giving scientists a glimpse of the universe that is far clearer than any telescope on Earth can. Since its launch in 1990, its discoveries have been used to write over 6,000 scientific papers, and it has helped scientists learn more about things like dark energy and gamma-ray bursts.

*CHEEESE!

Space Junk

Did you remember to **TAKE OUT THE TRASH** before you went to bed?

Trash pickups occur once or twice a week on this part of Earth, but who's collecting all of the trash and debris floating around space? This evening, as you're sleeping, there are more than 300,000 pieces of space junk orbiting the Earth. And this trash isn't just floating, it's flying through space at speeds of nearly 5 miles per second (7.7 kilometers per second)! What kind of junk is out there? Everything from tools, gloves, and screws dropped or misplaced by astronauts, to parts of satellites that have been broken off after being hit by other space junk. Even on Earth, we're not entirely safe. Old satellites and space junk regularly fall from space to the Earth's surface.

SPACE

Zzzzz Get Spaghettified

Things go **COMPLETELY DARK** when you fall asleep, but they brighten up again once you wake

up. Imagine going to a place so dark, no light can escape. It's impossible on Earth, but all over our universe, there are black holes sucking in everything—including light—in their gravitational pulls. If you were unfortunate enough to fall into a black hole and your friend remained outside, you would be able to see your friend as you fell into darkness, but your friend on the outside would not be able to see you, because nothing can escape a black hole, not even your image. Due to the intense gravitational pull of a black hole, it would have a stronger pull on your feet than on your head; this would stretch you like a piece of spaghetti!

SPACE

Mercury's Temperature Swings

We all know nighttime temperatures on Earth can get downright chilly, but nighttime temperatures on Mercury are OUT OF THIS WORLD! Because it's the closest planet to the sun, it should come as no surprise that temperatures on Mercury reach up to 800°F (430°C) during the day. But since the tiny planet has no atmosphere to hold in its heat, temperatures at night dip down to -280°F (-170°C). Be advised, if you're planning on having a slumber party on Mercury, don't just pack warm clothes, bring plenty of things to do: One 8-hour night on Mercury is about 19 Earth days long.

SPACE

Z Z Z Z Z # Are You Sirius?

Some dogs only come out in the black of night; Sirius, THE DOG STAR, is one such dog. The brightest star in the night sky, Sirius is so seriously bright, it is often mistaken for a UFO by people who have never seen it before. Not only is Sirius bright, it's a hot dog as well. Putting out 26 times more energy than our sun, Sirius's surface temperature is about 8,000°F (4,427°C) hotter than the sun. Best of all, it doesn't have to spend its nights alone. Shining next to it is its loyal companion, a smaller star called the Pup.

The Sun Never Sleeps

Even though it may **DIP OUT OF SIGHT** every night, the sun doesn't really go away, and it never takes a nap. It's constantly burning at around 10,000°F (5,500°C) on its surface and 27 *million*°F (15 million°C) at its core! What does it take to burn so hot? Lots and lots of fuel. It burns through more than 17 trillion tons (15 trillion metric tons) of fuel every Earth night! Even if you can't tell by staring at it, it's constantly growing. It's already big enough for over 1 million Earths to fit inside of it, and one day, it will grow big enough to swallow the Earth. But you can sleep easy, that won't happen for another 5 billion years.

Z
Z
Z
Z
Z

Rays Aren't Only for Days

Ever go out in the sun to "CATCH SOME RAYS"? You might not get as tan as during the day, but you are receiving rays at night as well. When the sun goes down, it takes its light rays with it, but the night sky is filled with plenty of stars, pulsars, and other outer-space objects that also send rays down to Earth. In addition to light rays (that are much weaker than the sun's, of course), they're sending radio, infrared, and ultraviolet rays. Fortunately, night and day, the Earth's atmosphere and magnetosphere protect us from becoming obliterated by all of these galactic rays.

Milky Way's Midnight Snack

Ever wake up HUNGRY in the middle of the night? You're not alone. At over 100,000 light-years across, with somewhere between 200 billion and 400 billion stars, and with a black hole at its center 4 *million* times more massive than our sun, the Milky Way galaxy has an out-of-this-world appetite. But what does a galaxy eat when it gets hungry? Other galaxies, of course. While you're sleeping (or midnight snacking), our galaxy is snacking on stars from the Sagittarius Dwarf Galaxy next to it. Since Sagittarius is about 10,000 times smaller than the Milky Way, there's little it can do as its stars get pulled into and torn apart by the Milky Way's gravitational pull.

Z Z Z Z Z

Andromeda Fast Approaching

When YOUR HEAD COLLIDES WITH YOUR PILLOW at night, it usually results in 8 hours of sleep.

But what do you think the outcome would be if two galaxies speeding toward each other at 270,000 miles per hour (432,000 kilometers per hour), one with 1 trillion stars, the other with over 200 billion stars, were to collide? It's not supposed to happen for another 3-5 billion years, but the Andromeda and Milky Way galaxies are on a collision course toward each other. Since there is so much space between the stars, you'd likely be able to sleep through most of the collision. However, the merging of the two galaxies' gravitational forces will likely knock several stars and planets off their current courses.

SPACE

Vampires from Outer Space

You may think that vampires exist only in your nightmares, but there is a whole classification of stars in outer space that are literally **DRAINING THE LIFE OUT OF OTHER STARS** in order to maintain their youthful appearances.

Scientists refer to these "vampire" stars as blue stragglers because they seem to straggle behind in age when compared to the other stars that surround them. But scientists have a theory as to how this happens. By draining hydrogen gas from nearby stars, blue stragglers are able to gain more fuel, become hotter, and remain brighter, younger-looking blue stars much longer.

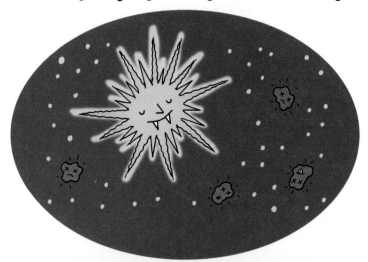

ZZ Z Z Z

The Mysterious Rays of the Universe

As much as they've learned about the universe, **WHEN ASTRONOMERS GO TO BED AT NIGHT,** they can do so with a lot of questions.

One of the biggest mysteries of our universe is what is responsible for nearly one-third of the detected 1,873 sources of gamma rays. Gamma rays are some of the most energized forms of light in the universe—a 10-second gamma burst gives off as much energy as our sun will in its 10-*billion*-year lifetime! Scientists have been able to track most gamma rays back to such powerful things as black holes and the explosions of giant stars. However, nearly 600 sources of gamma rays in our universe are unknown. Considering how powerful these sources must be, knowing more about them would help all of us sleep a little easier.

SPACE

Life on New Earth

While you were sleeping in 2009, astronomers discovered **A NEW PLANET.** They named the new planet Kepler 22b, but Earth Part II might have been a better name. In December 2011, it was discovered that, despite being roughly twice the size of Earth, Kepler 22b might be able to pass as Earth's twin. Just outside of our solar system, it's located in the Goldilocks Zone of a nearby star. Its location means its conditions are "just right" to have continents and oceans, similar to those on Earth, and where there is water, there can be life. But the best reason to dream of moving to Kepler 22b in the future? Its average temperature is 72°F (22°C).

Z z z z z Doughnut

In the wee morning hours, while you're still asleep, in large cities and small towns everywhere, **DOUGHNUTS** are being made by the **TENS OF THOUSANDS!** It's difficult to tell the exact number of doughnuts made, because the major chain doughnut makers like Krispy Kreme and Dunkin' Donuts aren't the only ones who get up to make them: There are thousands of small-town and independently owned doughnut shops. Which country eats the most doughnuts in the world? Canada.

Healthcare Workers

Every night you're dozing off, there are thousands of hospital workers **JUST STARTING THEIR "DAY."** Sicknesses and accidents can happen at any time, so healthcare workers need to be ready to work around the clock. This is wonderful for patients—and potential patients—but it creates a great inconvenience for the workers. Many nurses who work the night shift report having poor sleep habits. Just as troubling, as much as 25 percent of nighttime nurses report they stay awake for 24 hours the day before to prepare for their late-night shifts. This practice has shown an increase in accidents and mistakes.

Zzzzz Night Markets

While you're heading to bed each night, there are PEOPLE ALL OVER THE WORLD heading to the market. Many cities, from Chiang Mai, Thailand, to Lima, Peru, have markets that open up only after the sun goes down. Perhaps the most marvelous night market of them all can be found in Marrakech, Morocco. Locals and tourists stay up late and head to Djemaa el-Fna Square, where Marrakech's night market sets up shop. There's more to do there than just get stuffed on food. There are storytellers and musicians to hear and fortune-tellers to question. Tired of losing sleep looking for that "perfect" gift? Spells and curses can be purchased from the market's many magicians and snake charmers.

El Capitan

Ever have a hard time falling asleep because you were afraid there was **SOMETHING UNDER YOUR BED?** Try falling asleep with more than 1,000 feet (305 meters) of nothing below you. That's what it's like for the many adventure seekers who come from all over the world to climb Yosemite Park's El Capitan. Rising over 3,000 feet (914 meters) straight up, El Capitan is the world's largest solid granite monolith. Climbers must sleep at least one night attached to the rock wall. How do they catch their ZZZs without losing their grip on the rock wall? They use hammocklike beds, called bivouacs, that attach to the rock face. That way, they can fall asleep lying down just as if they were on the ground. Suddenly, your bedroom doesn't sound so frightening, does it?

ZZZZ Hide-and-Seek

What glows 630 feet (192 meters) high at night, is VIRTUALLY INVISIBLE during the day, and has lasers?

It's the lighting system for the Saint Louis Gateway Arch in Missouri. It must have been tough designing a system that was strong enough to illuminate such a massive monument without also blinding passing nighttime drivers. But lasers? Not only does the arch stand as a symbol of the United States' "Gateway to the West," it also stands as a gateway to one of the country's busiest nighttime migratory flyways. Since its bright lights, during cloudy or foggy nights, can cause birds to lose their direction or crash into the monument, lasers were installed to detect changes in the night sky, shutting off the lights when conditions are harmful for flying fowl.

The Statue of Liberty

LIBERTY NEVER SLEEPS, and neither does the torch that lights its way. Although the torch was designed to shine from the reflection of the sun's rays during the day, 16 floodlights are used to keep the Statue of Liberty's torch gleaming bright at night. Of course, Lady Liberty's flame's being covered in 24-karat gold also helps freedom bling. Her original torch can now be found in the lobby of the monument. It was removed in 1984 and replaced in 1986 with her current flame. However, the symbolism of it has never changed; it is intended to be an image of enlightenment, lighting the way to freedom.

ZZZZ Jelly Beans

Going to bed with a BELLY FULL of jelly beans?

Not recommended. But it is okay to go to sleep dreaming of attending the Jelly Belly University someday. Upon entering the university, outside of San Francisco, California, you'll be given a white lab coat and filled with loads of information before you "graduate" at the end. Too bad there's no final exam, because it's doubtful you'd have any trouble remembering any of the yummy details. From Geography: There are two other Jelly Belly factories in the world, one in Wisconsin, the other in Thailand. To History: The company was

started in 1869 by two German brothers, Gustav and Albert Goelitz. To Current Events: Making jelly beans is a 24-hour operation, but it takes from 7 to 21 days to make a single Jelly Belly jelly bean. So, it takes a week or more of sleep to equal a single, tasty bean.

Solar-Power Plant

Solar power is possibly the most ENVIRONMENTALLY FRIENDLY source of energy on Earth. Considering how hard it works all day long, it's hard to fault the sun for taking nights off. But just because the sun goes down doesn't mean people don't need energy. Luckily, scientists working for the Rice Solar Energy Project are working on a way to use the sun's power even at night. The secret? Molten salt. The proposed power plant will use 18,000 sun-catching mirrors to focus light onto a liquid salt mixture during the day. When the sun goes down, the machines will extract the energy from the salt to power a turbine that will generate energy for up to 7 hours a night.

POP CULTURE

Air Traffic Controller

You've heard of **COUNTING SHEEP TO HELP YOU GO TO SLEEP,** but airplanes? In spite of being a high-stress job, there have been several cases of air traffic controllers falling asleep during night shifts. And it's not necessarily because they're not getting enough sleep, either. Air traffic controllers are required to show up to work well rested, regardless of the time of their shift. However, studies show that night-shift workers—regardless of their jobs—can have difficulties staying awake if they don't keep active or mentally engaged. Since air traffic controllers working at night have fewer planes to land, and work in rooms surrounded by windows looking out at the night sky, they are particularly susceptible to falling asleep. Fortunately for fliers, new policies now allow controllers to read and listen to the radio in order to stay awake.

Computers Left On

Our world has become so automated, not every computer gets to TAKE A NIGHT OFF.

But for those that aren't necessary to keep the world running smoothly while we're asleep, it's a pretty good idea to switch them off. Every night, an estimated 54 million office PCs in the United States are not shut down properly. For every 10,000 computers left on overnight, American businesses are spending over $260,000 a year supplying energy to them. But it's not just the businesses that are paying: The amount of carbon dioxide put out from those 54 million computers is the equivalent of 4 million running cars! It turns out making sure your computer screen is black before you go to sleep is one of the easiest ways to make sure your planet (and wallet) is green when you wake up.

ZZzzz Tsunami Trash

While you're fast asleep, there's a 5-20-million-ton (5-18-metric-ton) "MONSTER" slowly making its way toward the United States' West Coast. No, it's not a 400-feet-tall (122-meter-tall) radioactive lizard; it's debris from Japan's earthquake and tsunami that occurred on March 11, 2011. The debris field is filled with just about anything that floats, including refrigerators, fishing boats, and wooden furniture. The objects were taken by the tsunami's waves and deposited into the ocean. In September 2011, the trash was sighted 2,000 miles (3,219 kilometers) from Japan, and it is expected to reach the United States sometime in 2014. So, you better get your sleep, because there's only a couple of years before it's time to take out some serious trash!

Nightly Navy Landings

Every night, **SOMEWHERE OVER THE OCEAN,** a navy pilot is making a landing on an aircraft carrier. Performing this landing has been described as "parking your car in a single-car garage in the dark of night at 120 miles per hour (193 kilometers per hour) with only a single little flashlight at the back of it to guide you in." Navy aviators are considered some of the best pilots in the world because of the skill involved in landing on a carrier. Now imagine piloting a plane on takeoff at night. The plane is catapulted down a runway approximately 300 feet (91 meters) long and, within 2 seconds, it's going about 200 miles per hour (324 kilometers per hour) into complete darkness. You wouldn't have any trouble staying awake on that flight!

Zzzzz Largest Lego Tower

The people of Brazil have just given their neighbors in Chile something other than an UPCOMING SOCCER MATCH to lose sleep over. In 2011, about 6,000 people in São Paulo, Brazil, most of whom were children, spent 4 days putting together 500,000 Lego pieces to construct the world's largest Lego tower. The 102-feet-tall (31-meter-tall) structure towers over the previous record holder, built in Santiago, Chile, the year before, by a whopping 9.8 inches (25 centimeters).

Late-Night Hunger

Just because the SUN GOES DOWN doesn't mean your hunger goes away.

Luckily for late-night munchers, there are plenty of places to get a meal at any time, day or night. In the United States alone, there are 1,600 Denny's restaurants serving breakfast, lunch, and dinner 24 hours a day. So, while you're "sawing logs" tonight, or snoring, there's surely someone somewhere cutting into a stack of pancakes. If it's a hankering for a nice jellyfish salad or sea snails in garlic sauce that's got you up all night, then swing by the Great NY Noodletown in New York City's Chinatown. It's open until early morning and is a favorite spot for New York chefs to grab a bite after they close their own kitchens.

Zzzzz Racing All Day and Night

The threat of falling asleep while driving is always scary, but cruising around a track over 200 miles per hour (322 kilometers per hour) should be enough to **SCARE ANY DRIVER AWAKE.** Every year, in Le Mans, France, race-car drivers give their best shots at staying awake during the 24 Hours of Le Mans race. Luckily, the cars in the race are driven by teams of three, rather than one driver per car. That way, racers can break up the time they spend with their hands on the wheels with the time spent with their heads on pillows. By the end of the race, cars will cover distances up to 3,235 miles (5,206 kilometers).

Rock Yourself Awake

You've heard of **ROCKING YOURSELF TO SLEEP,** but rocking yourself awake? That's exactly what Suresh Joachim did for 75 hours and 3 minutes from August 24 to 27 in 2005, when he set the world record for most time continuously rocking in a rocking chair. But staying awake isn't strange for Suresh; he's set over 30 world records, including standing on one foot for 76 hours and 40 minutes, dancing for 400 hours, and going up and down an escalator for 7 days. So, what are you doing tonight?

Night Surfing

Normally, the **"SURF'S UP"** when you're up, but there's a new surfing competition that you've most likely been sleeping through. Started in 2010, on Florida's Flagler Beach, Red Bulls Night Riders is a new surfing event that has competitors flying over waves under the stars. Illuminated by bright lights and a full moon, surfers must adapt to the otherwise dark conditions to successfully land their surf-jumping stunts. In 2011, over 6,000 spectators watched surfing veteran Cody Thompson take home the top prize.

The Subways That Never Sleep

While most of the people in **New York City** are getting some shut-eye, its subway trains **KEEP ON ROLLING** throughout the night. It takes over 6,000 cars and 660 miles (1,062 kilometers) of track to transport the city's population of over 8 million around all five of its boroughs. In 2010, the trains carried a total of 1.6 billion of the city's citizens and visitors a distance of about 347 million miles (559 million kilometers)—all without a single night off!

All-Night Bike Class

ZZZZZ

You've probably been fortunate enough never to have PULLED AN ALL-NIGHTER. Chances are, when you head to college, you won't be so lucky. But what if it were your class that lasted all night? Since 1974, Columbia University professor Kenneth Jackson has taught an all-night class on the history of New York City. How is he able to cover so much material in a single night? The entire class takes place while riding bikes. Getting around the busy city can be tricky during the day, but biking through the streets of New York at night offers a unique and gridlock-free view of the city. The class begins at 11:30 p.m. on Columbia's campus in Manhattan and finishes after 6 a.m. in Brooklyn.

Days That Never Finish

If you have trouble falling asleep with the lights on, **GOOD LUCK GETTING ANY SHUT-EYE** in Finland during the summer. As in other countries that reach up to the Arctic Circle, the sun never fully sets in Finland during the summertime. Finns take full advantage of their extra light each year by celebrating Juhannus on the third Saturday of June. Juhannus is the name of their midsummer festival, and the traditional way to celebrate it is to visit a cabin on a lake and build huge bonfires. They also have several superstitions associated with this all-day sunlight. One is that if you sleep with nine different flowers under your pillow, you will dream of your future love.

When Duty Calls

Just because you're SAFELY ASLEEP IN YOUR HOME, it doesn't mean emergencies aren't happening elsewhere. Every night, thousands of firefighters stay awake just in case a disaster strikes. It's a good thing, too, because about one-third of all fatal residential building fires in the United States occur between midnight and 5 a.m. This doesn't mean that every night is full of excitement for all of those firemen and firewomen; firefighters actually respond to more false alarms than real fires.

A Glow in One

Ever since the invention of the lightbulb, sports have become 24-HOUR ACTIVITIES, with the exception of golf. It would cost way too much money to light up an entire golf course, right? Right. But that hasn't stopped many people from going golfing when they should be going to bed. With glow sticks to identify players and golf bags, and with players whacking glow-in-the-dark golf balls, night golf is catching on. It's especially popular in places such as Arizona, where daytime temperatures are so high, nighttime is the only time cool enough to play a round.

Zzzz Night of Fire

For five days every March, the people of Valencia, Spain, take part in one of the BIGGEST PARTIES ON THE PLANET, Las Fallas. Each day starts out with fireworks being tossed throughout the streets, but the festival's most noticeable attractions aren't the loud noises; they're the giant *ninots* standing on neighborhood corners. *Ninots* are larger-than-life dolls, made out of wood and paper, that make fun of politicians, celebrities, and other famous people. With many reaching over 20 feet (6 meters) in height, the *ninots'* participation in the festival is temporary. On the last night of the festival, they're stuffed with fireworks and at midnight, the *ninots* are set on fire to burn until early morning.

Dead Asleep

HALLOWEEN IS A FAVORITE NIGHT of the year for many, but did you know it's been around for a couple thousand years? Just as amazingly, many of its traditions haven't changed much, like dressing up in strange costumes and telling stories about ghosts. Long before kids started asking neighbors for candy, the Celts of Britain believed that on November 1, the ghosts of the dead returned to the land of the living. The tradition of wearing costumes grew out of the belief that wearing a mask would keep ghosts from knowing who you were if you had to leave your house on Halloween. Asking for treats from your neighbors comes from the belief that leaving a bowl of food outside your home would keep the ghosts from coming inside.

Zzzzz Night Teeth

Did you ever put your tooth under your pillow for the TOOTH FAIRY, before going to bed? Wonder where it went? Wonder where the tooth fairy came from? It's possible the tooth fairy was originally a mouse. At least, according to the 18th-century French fairy tale "La Bonne Petite Souris," this good fairy would turn into a mouse so she could hide under pillows and tease an evil king, to later knock out all of his teeth. The tooth fairy didn't make it to the United States until the early 20th century. Once she did, she no longer turned into a mouse or fought a nasty king; she focused only on putting money under pillows in exchange for baby teeth.

Extra Hour

Z Z Z Z Z

Who wouldn't like an extra hour of sleep? **TOO BAD IT HAPPENS ONLY ONCE A YEAR.** Each fall, when daylight saving time ends, people all over the world set their clocks back an hour before going to bed. However, not every country in the world and not every state in the United States observes daylight saving time, so it really depends on where you fall asleep. The purpose of setting the clocks back is to increase the amount of daylight available in the evening. The hope is that, with more daylight in the evening, people won't need to turn on their lights as early and will thus use less energy while they're awake.

POP CULTURE

ZZZzz Lights at Night

While you're sleeping, **THERE ARE STREETLIGHTS ON ALL OVER THE WORLD**, but that hasn't always been the case. Streetlights date back to the ancient Chinese, who used leaking volcanic gas contained in bamboo tubes. The Romans were also known to use vegetable oil to light some streets. The first public streetlights to use gas in Europe were turned on in London, United Kingdom, in 1807. A special nighttime job was created to maintain these lights—a lamplighter. This was a person who walked a city at night, turning on all of the streetlights, but the job did not last long. By 1857, La Rue Imperiale, in Lyons, France, became the first street to be lit using electric lights. Today, solar-powered streetlights are available.

All Night at the Museum

Every year since 1977, MUSEUM FANS HAVE CELEBRATED International Museum Day. But no matter how much people loved museums, they could only enjoy them during the day. That all changed in 2005, when European museum visitors began celebrating their admiration of artifacts by taking an evening off sleep to visit their favorite museums at night. In 2011, several thousand museums in 40 different European countries participated by offering free admission and keeping their doors open until early morning hours. So far, there have been no reports of exhibits coming to life.

Nights and Days Across the Globe

The WORLD SPINS and we keep busy. Whenever a child on the West Coast of the United States gets ready for bed at 9 p.m., there's a child getting ready for school in Cairo, Egypt, because over there, it's 7 a.m. Due to the Earth's rotation, we don't all share the same days and nights. So, if you're on the East Coast, when your parents are getting into work around 9 a.m., parents in Beijing, China, are probably getting to bed at 10 p.m.

The Night the Lights Go Out in Vegas

Z Z Z Z Z

Normally, IT'S HARD TO SAY EXACTLY HOW MANY BULBS are lighting up Las Vegas, Nevada, but for one night every year, the number drops to zero. For 1 hour in March, Las Vegas goes dark to observe Earth Hour. Earth Hour is an international effort to bring attention to global warming and energy conservation. By turning off all lights and appliances for 1 hour during the evening, organizers hope to encourage people to turn things off when they're not being used. Just as your body needs to shut down and go dark for a few hours every night, the Earth could use a rest as well!

POP CULTURE

Another Reason to Behave During the Day

ZZZZZ

If you're ever in South Africa or Swaziland, make sure you behave yourself, because **IF YOU DON'T,** Tokoloshe might "get you" in your sleep. Who is Tokoloshe? According to Zulu mythology, he's a little, hairy, dwarflike creature that sneaks into people's bedrooms at night to cause trouble. While there have been no confirmed sightings of Tokoloshe, many people in the countries of southern Africa still put their beds on a stack of bricks in order to raise them up so Tokoloshe can't reach them while they're sleeping.

All-Night House

Some people may think **WAFFLES ARE ONLY FOR BREAKFAST,** but that's because they've never been to a **Waffle House** at night. The more than 1,500 **Waffle Houses** across the United States have over 145 reasons to stay open 24 hours a day. That's how many waffles they serve every minute. And, in order to help people stay awake to enjoy all of those waffles, they serve enough coffee in a year to fill eight Olympic-size swimming pools. If that's not enough to make you dream about breakfast, consider this: Every day, **Waffle House** restaurants serve enough sausage patties that, stacked on top of one another, they would be four times taller than the Empire State Building!

ZZZZ Texas Stadium

SUPER BOWL XLV, held at the Cowboys Stadium in Dallas, Texas, almost came to be remembered as the Ice Bowl. Days before Super Bowl Sunday, Dallas was hit with a monster winter storm that left snow and ice everywhere, including the top of the state-of-the-art Cowboys Stadium. Before the big game, ice sliding off the stadium injured six people. To prevent further injury, 30 firefighters were asked to become ice fighters for a night. They stayed up all night before the Super Bowl, breaking up the ice with fire hoses. Between their efforts and the heat of the next morning's sun, the stadium was safe enough to pack in 103,219 spectators to watch Green Bay steal a win from Pittsburgh.

Robots at Night

Working at night is SOOO 20TH CENTURY. In the near future, many jobs people now do overnight will be performed by robots. Robotics engineers are already working on robots that can clean floors of office buildings after workers have left for the evening. In 2012, South Korea introduced its first robot prison guards. Scientists are even studying how bats use echolocation to navigate at night to help them design robots that can move as smoothly in the dark as they do during the day.

Zzzzz Run Yourself Awake

You've heard of sleepwalking, but

SLEEP RUNNING?

If only the runners in the Bighorn Trail Run were that lucky. Even though the race can take a full day to complete, the participants in this endurance race are way too busy covering its 100-mile (161-kilometer) course to take a break. Why would anyone give up sleep to run for more than 20 consecutive hours? This ultramarathon was started in 2002 to commemorate the 10th anniversary of three shorter runs that take place in the Bighorn Mountains of Wyoming. Those three races were started to increase awareness of the natural beauty of the area, especially in the face of development projects that were threatening to alter it. So far, nature lovers and runners can rest easy as the proposed development project has not been implemented.

Wind Power

Solar power is great, but
WHAT ABOUT AT NIGHT?

Its power source is gone. What naturally occurring source of energy is available night and day? Wind. Many states in the United States are starting to turn to wind power to make up for their lack of coal, natural gas, or other forms of fossil fuels. Minnesota, for example, has gotten so good at harnessing the wind that passes over its plains, it has begun exporting some of the wind energy to neighboring states. So, while you're sleeping tonight, there are giant wind turbines spinning all over fields of corn and soybeans in Minnesota in order to provide power in the morning.

POP CULTURE

Late-Night Skiing

Z Z Z Z Z

Do you find skiing during the daytime NOT CHALLENGING enough?

Then you should skip your shut-eye and try skiing with the lights out. Ski resorts across the globe are offering an exciting alternative to traditional ski runs—night skiing. In addition to costing less than daytime skiing, hitting the slopes while most are hitting the hay gives skiers a less crowded experience. The adventure of night skiing varies from resort to resort. While most resorts offer some form of lighting on their ski runs, the Zermatt resort in Switzerland leaves only moonlight and the twinkling of stars to guide nighttime skiers.

Apps

While you're dreaming in bed, someone is surely DREAMING UP the next app. Between 2008 and 2011, the Apple App Store alone had more than 18 *billion* downloads. Google's Android Market also announced it had hit 3 billion app downloads by the end of 2011. Combined, that's just under one app for every person on the planet! And none of the apps is worth much without something to show them on. Every night you're asleep, there are over 500,000 new Android phones being activated around the world.

ZZZZZ Tweet Sleep

Throughout a typical day in 2011, 144 MILLION TWEETS ARE POSTED ON TWITTER.

That's about 48 million posted while you're sleeping. Not everyone complains about not being able to sleep. They're too busy staying up, checking out what's going on. While it took a little over 3 years for the 1 billionth Tweet, there are now more than 1 billion Tweets every week. So far, the record for most Tweets per second (TPS) was 6,939. It was set 4 seconds past midnight in Japan, on New Year's Day 2012.

Iditarod, But I Didn't Sleep ᶻᶻᶻᶻᶻ

During **ALASKA'S ANNUAL MUSHING MARATHON,** the Iditarod Trail Sled Dog Race, mushers guide their sleds, pulled by teams of dogs, over 1,150 miles (1,851 kilometers) of snow and ice.

It takes about 9 days to finish the race, but not a lot of sleeping takes place. Race rules require competitors to make at least three stops (two 8-hour stops and one 24-hour stop) to check the health of the dogs. The rest of the nights are spent out in the cold Alaskan landscape. Many racers sleep only 2 hours, while dogs typically get 6 hours of sleep for every 6 hours they're pulling the sled.

Z Z Z Z Z

A Nervous Night's Sleep

Have trouble sleeping? TRY SLEEPING AT THE TOP OF A VOLCANO. Located between Los Angeles and Las Vegas in Newberry Springs, California, is what looks like a crash-landed flying saucer on the top of a cinder-cone volcano. It's a house! The home, owned by television personality Huell Howser, is completely surrounded by glass walls and has an observation deck on top that gives a 360-degree view of the surrounding desert, which looks remarkably like a lunar landscape. That's amazing!

Source Notes

2005 Aichi Expo
ABC News
About.com
Accuweather.com
All About Animals
allyosemite.com
Almanac.com
American Wildlife Foundation
America's Wetland Foundation
Amphibian and Reptile Conservation
Amphibiaweb.org
Animal Planet
Archlighting.com
Arizona State University
Articlesbase.com
Artisanbreadbaking.com
Astrononmy.com
Astrosociety.org
Australian Government Department of Affairs and Trade
BBC
Better Homes and Gardens
Bighorn Mountain Wild and Scenic Trail Run
Bioart.co.uk
Biobay.com
Biodiversityexplorer.org
Bioone.org
Birdorable.com
Bitsandpieces.us
Brainmuseum.org
Brighthub.com
Bristishwildboard.org
Britannica.com
CBC News
CBS News
California Department of Fish and Game
California Energy Commission
California Institute of Technology
Camelspider.org
Careerbuilder.com
Center for Educational Technologies
Chipper Woods Bird Observatory
Christian Science Monitor
Cloudedleopard.org
CNN

College of Saint Benedict and Saint John's University
Colorado State University
Columbia Daily Spectator
Contexttravel.com
Coolquiz.com
Cooperative Institute for Marine and Atmospheric Studies
Coral-reef-info.com
Cornell University
Dailygalaxy.com
Daily Mail (U.K.)
Dallas Morning News
Defenders.org
Denny's
Dentalgentlecare.com
Desertmusuem.org
Desertusa.com
Dictionary.com
Digitaljournal.com
Discover (magazine)
Discovery Channel
Distancebetweencities.net
Dlc.fi
Donquijote.com
Ehow.com
Enature.com
EQtravelphotography.com
ESPN
Earthsky.org
Earthtrust.org
Emedicinehealth.com
Enchantedlearning.com
Encyclopedia of Earth
Environmentalgraffiti.com
Essortmant.com
Eurekaalert.org
European Space Agency
Eyecare Educators
Extremescience.com
Fairfax County Public Schools
Fastcompany.com
Ferring Pharmaceuticals
Findingdulcinea.com
Finland.org
Fire.org
Fishbase.org

Flyingmag.com
Franklin Institute
Fresh-energy.org
Fultonsun.com
Galaxydynamics.org
Gardening.online-business-idea.com
Geekwire.com
Grindtv.com
Guinness World Records
Happynews.com
Harvard Medical School
Highlights Kids
History.com
Honeybadger.com
Honolulu Zoo
HowStuffWorks
Howard Hughes Medical Institute
Hubblesite.org
Huffingtonpost.com
Indiana University
International Council of Museums
Jellybelly.com
Johnstonarchive.net
Johns Hopkins University Applied Physics Laboratory
Joyofplants.com
KSDK.com
Kentucky Injury Prevention and Research Center
Kew.org
Kidshealth.org
Las Vegas Sun
Library of Congress
Livestrong.com
Livescience.com
Livingrainforest.org
Lonelyplanet.com
Mathisfun.com
MIT News
MSNBC
MTA
Marinebio.org
Maryland Department of Natural Resources
Maryland Zoo
MayoClinic.com
Medicinenet.com

Index